Alfred J. Cohen

Familiar Chats with the Queens of the Stage

Alfred J. Cohen
Familiar Chats with the Queens of the Stage
ISBN/EAN: 9783337322670
Printed in Europe, USA, Canada, Australia, Japan
Cover: Foto ©ninafisch / pixelio.de

More available books at **www.hansebooks.com**

FAMILIAR CHATS

WITH THE

QUEENS OF THE STAGE.

BY

ALAN DALE,

AUTHOR OF

"A MARRIAGE BELOW ZERO," "AN EERIE HE AND SHE," ETC., ETC.

> "When in the chronicle of wasted time,
> I see descriptions of the fairest wights,
> And beauty making beautiful old rime,
> In praise of ladies dead, and lovely knights,
> Then in the blazon of sweet beauty's best,
> Of hand, of foot, of lip, of eye, of brow,
> I see their antique pen would have expressed
> Even such a beauty as you master now."
> —*Shakespeare.*

NEW YORK:
COPYRIGHT, 1890, BY

G. W. Dillingham, Publisher,

SUCCESSOR TO G. W. CARLETON & CO.

MDCCCXC.

All Rights Reserved.

TO

LEANDER RICHARDSON,

UNDER WHOSE GUIDING AND STOUTLY FEATHERED WING I
FIRST SAW THE LAND THAT MOST OF THE STAGE
QUEENS, HERE DISCUSSED, CLAIM AS
THEIR OWN,

I DEDICATE THIS VOLUME IN ALL GRATITUDE.

ALAN DALE.

CONTENTS.

INTRODUCTION
LILLIAN RUSSELL
MRS. JAMES BROWN-POTTER
ROSE COGHLAN
FANNY DAVENPORT
LOTTA
HELENA MODJESKA
ISABELLE URQUHART
SADIE MARTINOT
GEORGIA CAYVAN
MRS. LANGTRY
MARY ANDERSON
AGNES BOOTH
MINNIE PALMER

Emma Juch	195
Marie Jansen	205
Marie Wainwright	223
Louise Beaudet	233
Pauline Hall	247
Marion Manola	259
Effie Ellsler	273
Mrs. D. P. Bowers	287
Ada Rehan	301
Georgie Drew Barrymore	311
Little Gertie Homan	321
Lilly Post	333
Ellen Terry	345
Clara Morris	353
Rosina Vokes	375
Nellie McHenry	385

ILLUSTRATIONS.

	Page
LILLIAN RUSSELL	*Frontispiece*
MRS. JAMES BROWN-POTTER	57
ROSE COGHLAN	70
FANNY DAVENPORT	84
LOTTA	93
HELENA MODJESKA	106
ISABELLE URQUHART	118
SADIE MARTINOT	130
GEORGIA CAYVAN	140
MRS. LANGTRY	153
MARY ANDERSON	164
AGNES BOOTH	174
MINNIE PALMER	186
EMMA JUCH	196

	Page
Marie Jansen	205
Marie Wainwright	224
Louise Beaudet	234
Pauline Hall	247
Marion Manola	260
Effie Ellsler	274
Mrs. D. P. Bowers	288
Ada Rehan	301
Georgie Drew Barrymore	312
Little Gertie Homan	322
Lilly Post	334
Ellen Terry	345
Rosina Vokes	376
Nellie McHenry	386

INTRODUCTION.

LET nobody who takes up this book for perusal, imagine that I am about to assume the rôle of a biographer, or that I have the very smallest ambition in that direction. I am afraid that I could never be a Boswell to anybody's Johnson, for the simple reason that I was born without the bump of veneration. Pity me, kind readers, all of whom, I sincerely trust, are possessed of every beautiful phrenological attribute known to Dr. Gall. The ability to venerate is a delightful gift; the inability a veritable disaster, bringing forth enemies by the score. I always envy the man who can

find a hero or a heroine without any difficulty. He is a brother of the lucky individual who accepts exquisite intentions for indifferent deeds. These people are of distinct value to the community. They are some of the wheels that help to move society. Everybody likes them. You have heard of the lady who pathetically and melodiously remarked, "Oh, would I were a bird!" Well, I have always felt inclined to adapt this to myself, and to exclaim "Oh, would I were a wheel!"

What a flamboyantly felicitous individual he must be who can see Edwin Booth as *Hamlet* one night, and James Owen O'Connor in the same rôle the next night, and yet find kind words to say of either! Picture to yourself the paradisaical life of him who can gush ecstatically over Mme. Sarah Bernhardt in "La Tosca," and still find that his adjectival eloquence has not been exhausted when he witnesses the performance of Miss Fanny Davenport in the same play. There are many such. I have met them, and they have been more wonderful to me than any dime museum freaks. I have broken the tenth commandment time after time. Whenever I have come in contact with any of these bits of human sunshine I have coveted their priceless possession—the bump of veneration. I have yearned for it. I have tried to cultivate it, but have come to the conclusion that I might as well attempt to grow an apple tree in a bag of sawdust.

Now a man who tries to deal biographically with a score of actresses ought to be a person literally saturated with the milk of human kindness, otherwise he will be absolutely unable to keep comparisons and opinions from his work. If the same person write the lives of Ada Rehan and Estelle Clayton, with anything more than the dates of the production of the various plays in which they have appeared, he will, unless he be one of the rose-tinted creatures to whom I have referred, surely give offence to one of the ladies. Miss Rehan may sue him for libelous ridicule ; Miss Clayton may ask her manager to interview him with a club for derogatory statements. I do not mean to say that the discreet individual is not to be found who could evasively satisfy both ladies, and still avoid being rose-tinted. But I do dare to assert that such biographies will be singularly uninteresting to the non-theatrical public.

When my publisher, Mr. Dillingham, asked me for sketches of a number of actresses whom he named, I trembled in my shoes. I thought he meant biographies, and the horror of becoming a theatrical biographer almost overwhelmed me. Then came the joyous information that biographies were not necessary. All that was wanted was a series of gossipy sketches, or interviews, or notes, to which Mr. Dillingham would supply some charming pictures. His task, I realized, was an easier one than mine. He got the lovely faces—I, the careers they have helped to make. Not a soul can object to his beautiful and costly photogravures, while I may be clubbed out of existence and twenty irate ladies may dance a *can-can* on my grave. But I do not repine. I frankly admit that there is more of Dillingham than of Dale in this book, and that his work is better in every respect than mine.

For some years I have had a great deal to do with actors and actresses, in the shape of interviewing, criticising, paragraphing. They have been happy years for me. I have met some of the most entertaining people in the world, some of the queerest, some of the most ridiculous, some of the most amusing.

At the risk of being considered egotistical, I must say that I think my experience with the ladies and gentlemen of the stage has been as acute as that of anybody I know. While most of the metropolitan critics sit at their desks all day, and see the people they criticise at night only, it has been my lot to meet actors and actresses in the day-time and criticise them at night. Even my enemies will admit that my criticisms have been as frank and out-spoken as any in New York. Picture the condition of the man who condemns an actor in vigorous terms in a criticism, and meets him with a smiling face the next day, expecting to be well received.

I assure you, my readers, that there have been days when I dreaded to present myself on Broadway; when visions of outraged actors and avenging pistols have forced themselves upon me. But I have never absented myself, and I still live to tell the tale. I have discovered that nearly every actor and actress writhes in agony at the very suggestion of condemnation; an insinuation is sufficient to throw them into ecstasies of indignation. On the other hand, they receive praise ungraciously and disappointingly, as though it were their due. Nobody despises the universal gusher more thoroughly than the actor, yet nobody is more furious if he change his rôle. That sounds paradoxical, does it not? It is a fact, however.

Once upon a time, I had a great admirer in a young actor, who never let an opportunity of showering upon me fulsome compliments escape him. I had never seen him act.

"Alan," he said to me one day, "do you know I couldn't get on if I were not able to read your criticisms. I have them forwarded to me whenever I leave town."

Of course I was profoundly touched by this example of unbounded appreciation. Every man likes to hear pleasant things said of himself— even if he isn't an actor. A few months later this amiable youth was cast for a part in a metropolitan production. It was my duty to criticise the production. I did so. My appreciative friend was simply atrocious. If he had been my brother I should have hated his performance just the same. I came out next day with my honest views, and then forgot all about the matter. A couple of weeks after this I met the young actor and shook hands with him. He was so cold that he chilled me to the very marrow.

"I am awfully sorry," he said, "that you have stopped writing criticisms."

I looked at him in amazement. "You are mistaken," I remarked; "I am still at my old post."

"Well," he declared, "I repeat that you have stopped writing criticisms. You don't criticise any more. That stuff you indulge in is simply a cruel attempt to undermine the careers of those before the public."

Ye gods! The charge almost took away my breath. I felt that it was my duty to be indignant, but I couldn't fulfil my duty. The ridiculous side of the situation struck me so forcibly that I roared with laughter. When I had composed myself I found that I was alone.

My indignant friend was striding down the avenue, freighted with his wrath.

On one occasion an actor informed me that he had a little play that was to be produced at a city theatre. If it proved to be a success, he intended sending it out for a tour of the country; if it were not a success—well, there would be nothing lost.

" Now, my dear fellow," he said, " I particularly want you to come and see it. If you like it, say so; if you don't like it, please don't hesitate to express your opinion for the sake of any kindly feelings you may have towards myself."

That was a very neat way of putting it, was it not? The privilege of saying that I didn't like the play in case it proved objectionable, was surely a delicate piece of consideration. The performance took place in due course. How sincerely I hoped that it might prove worthy. The first act was so prodigiously awful that everybody in the theatre appeared to be laughing. The play was a tragedy. I tried to believe that it was a farce, and to like it as such. Impossible! As a tragedy the play was bewildering; as a farce, it was a piece of prosy stupidity. I went home and said exactly what I thought about it. All the other papers roasted it, but the actor seemed to single me out for his particular ire. He did not visit me, thank goodness! but he vilified me to all my friends. I was incapable of criticism; I was corrupt; I was an absurdity, and so forth and so on. Yet I had merely done what he asked me to do. I had said I didn't like the play because I didn't.

Not unfrequently actors and actresses use diplomatic methods to express their disapproval of your criticisms. They write anonymous letters or pen effusions signed, "An admirer of Mr. So-and-So," "A friend of justice," or (when they want to be particularly insinuating), "One of your most appreciative readers."

In a play I went to see not very long ago, a

very good-looking English actor appeared. His dramatic value was of less consequence than his good looks. His Adonisian qualities were invariably emphasized. I said something to that effect. Two days later I received a letter signed " An English Girl."

"After reading your article," wrote my correspondent, "I went to see the play. You are always bright and witty, but are you not a little hard on Mr. Blank, and isn't it rather shabby of you to take him so continually for your victim? Surely there are other English actors here whom you can pick to pieces equally as much as Mr. Blank—for instance, Wilson Barrett, Terriss, the beautiful (?) Conway, and lots of others equally faulty. I was surprised to see Mr. Blank act so well. I don't think you should blame him for being good-looking, but attribute that to America for producing such ugly men. Isn't it only natural that American girls, seeing only plain men, should set up Mr. Blank for an

Adonis? You may walk the avenue and find hundreds of pretty girls, but *they* can't find ten good-looking men unless among the actors, and then they are English. Your articles, Mr. Alan Dale, are always well written and amusing, and we look forward to them; but take my advice and 'let up' on Mr. Blank for a bit. Pick some one else to pieces and then when you go back to him (as I see he is your stand-by), your articles will be read with more interest, for then they won't be so stale, or (pardon me) 'chestnutty.'"

Now, I feel perfectly sure that the writer of this entertaining letter was none other than Mr. Blank himself, or one of his most acute friends, who had taken up the pen at his instigation. Had I written six volumes of warmest praise, I should never have heard from him. He would have accepted it as his due without a murmur.

One night I went to see a new play at a down-town theatre. The piece did not possess much dramatic value, but some of the "specialties" introduced were excellent. The dancing of one young man was so clever and unusual, that it impressed me greatly. I praised him rather enthusiastically next day. He was an oasis of entertainment in a desert of rubbish. Two or three days later I was introduced to him.

"I have been wanting to meet you," he said fervently, "to thank you for the kindest words that have ever been applied to a performance of mine. I shall be grateful to you for life."

I assured him that there was no reason for this luminous gratitude. I had merely done my duty. I had expressed my sincere opinion, a task which I was paid to perform. He shook my hand, and almost wept on my bosom. I earnestly wished I had been worthy of his enthusiasm, and began to realize that there must be a great deal of sweetness in doing a genuinely benevolent act. I knew, however, that there was no benevolence in this.

The following Christmas-day I was dumfounded to receive a box containing a Christmas card and a beautiful pair of white satin braces. There was not a word in the parcel explanatory of its source. I tortured my brains to discover the donor, but without any success. I took the braces home, and showed them to my wife. She was fearfully indignant.

"So those horrible actresses have been sending you braces—braces, of all things in the world," she remarked, furiously. "Oh! of course you are pleased. I might have expected that. I wonder what you'll get next. Braces! A more suggestive and brazen present I couldn't imagine. Who sent them?"

I answered feebly that I had no idea on that subject. That made her still more irate.

"No idea?" she sneered. "Well, I have. Put them on at once. Pray, don't mind me."

I gave the braces away next day. I found a friend who wanted a pair, and who had never dreamed of anything so lovely as white satin. A few days later I received a letter from Chicago.

"I am a trifle disappointed," it ran, "at no acknowledgment of my letter, or the box I sent. I know it didn't amount to much, but I wanted you to know that I appreciated your kindness."

I had received no previous letter. I looked at the signature of this one. It came from the enthusiastic young actor whose dancing I had praised. I almost foamed at the mouth. It was so annoying to receive a present from a comparative stranger, and under such ridiculous circumstances!

The next time I saw him was in a comic opera that proved to be a terrible *fiasco*. He did as well as he could with a bad part. I said this and nothing more. I met him next day and there were "braces" in his eyes.

"That was very unkind," he said. "I think you *might* have said something nice about me." He looked as though he meant to add "under the bracing circumstances of the case."

Some time ago I received a letter from an actor whom I had met, enclosing me tickets for a performance which he was most anxious to have criticised. "I hope that my performance," he said, "may please you. I think you will find that all actors admire your criticisms, even though you bring them up with a round turn, for they believe what you say is what you think, and respect you, as a man, for your honesty. I believe that the critic, who, without prejudice, shows you your bad faults," (bad faults is excellent) "is the best friend a man can have who wishes to become an artist. I will close by saying that I hope at some future time to have the pleasure of taking you by the hand."

Well, I went to see this amiable youth, and I admired his performance immensely. It was really an excellent piece of work. But he was playing a part that had been created by an actor of reputation, and he imitated this actor in an amazingly servile manner, even indulging in the peculiar mispronunciation of certain words that his predecessor had favored. I praised the young man very warmly, but I spoke of the servile imitation, and deplored it. It was totally unnecessary. A few days later I received a letter from my unseen friend. The good things I had said of him were comparatively unnoticed. The imitation business had evidently wounded his sweet, sensitive nature. I am convinced that, at this moment, he is not nearly so anxious to take me by the hand.

I used to find great difficulty in answering that much vexed problem: Would you sooner look a greater fool than you are, or be one? I can answer it now. I would sooner be a greater fool than I am, for experience has taught me that it would be impossible for me to look a greater fool than I look. A nice, meek, gentlemanly young idiot, is what many theatrical people take me to be. I have seen this again and again. As I am perfectly convinced that I am not an idiot I am forced to believe that I must look like one, and the reason is this: I listen to what every man or woman has to say, and maintain a resolute silence. If I am obliged to speak I generally acquiesce. If an actor tells me that he is the greatest artist on earth, I let him think that I have accepted his statement. If an actress deluge me with eloquence on the subject of her remarkable impersonation, I smile happily and seem to agree with her. If, later on, I see this actor and actress on the stage, and dislike their performance, I say so. That surprises them. They had come to believe that I had no opinions of my own, and that they had carefully impregnated me with their own views. When next I meet them, they are very cold, and very amazed. This has happened a hundred times within the last five years. It is only by adverse criticism that the eccentricities of dramatic people come to the surface.

Some years ago, I was living in a little French boarding-house in West Twelfth street. It wasn't at all swell, and it was for that reason that I selected it. My purse lacked *embonpoint*. This boarding-house suited its emaciated state very nicely. In this place I met the little lady who was once queen of the comic opera stage in America. She is dead now. I suppose I may as well give her name. It was Marie Aimée. She stayed at the West Twelfth street house when in the city. She lived there expensively, and everybody adored her. I have never since met so charming a little woman. Aimée had a heart as large as her reputation. She was, moreover, an artist to the finger tips. She has had many imitators, but they have fallen far short of the original.

One day I thought that I would write a short

article on Aimée in this boarding-house. I did so. I pictured her daintily smoking the after-dinner cigarette, surrounded by the admiring folks of the establishment, who were all fighting for a place in her good graces. The article was published. The next day, when I presented myself at table, there was dead silence. I was absolutely ignored. I spoke of the weather, but my remarks were unheeded. I passed the pickles, but they were declined without thanks. I soon became distinctly uncomfortable. Next day I was approached by Mme. Hortense, the landlady.

"Sir," she said, "you have tried deliberately to harm me, and I shall never forgive you. You have written an article that makes us all ridiculous, and if you can find it convenient to look for other quarters, I shall esteem it a favor."

There was only one word to express my sensations. It is not pretty, but I shall use it. I was flabbergasted. For some minutes I could not speak.

"Madame," I said, when I had partly recovered, "I assure you I said nothing in my article to which anybody could reasonably take offence. Please tell me wherein I have sinned?"

She cast upon me a look of withering scorn. "It is easily told," she remarked. "I will say nothing of the anger of my two Belgian boarders, who of course recognize themselves in the caricature you have made of 'two bald-headed dudes.' They can fight their own battles. You have, however, insulted Mme. Aimée. You alluded to her as smoking cigarettes. She is furious, and so am I. Do you imagine that I would permit any woman to smoke cigarettes in *my* house?"

I hesitated for a moment. The cigarettes *had* been smoked, and I did not see why I should allow myself to be brow-beaten without any defence.

"Surely I saw Mme. Aimée smoking"—I began meekly.

The meekness was all on my side.

"Supposing you did?" declared my landlady, with strength enough for us both. "It was not necessary to say so. I do not court newspaper notoriety, and I will not have it."

I packed up my goods and chattels next day and departed. I did not discuss the subject with Aimée at the time, but I subsequently heard that she did not mind the cigarette affair in the least. Her sole objection to the article was that I had mentioned the fact that she lived in a boarding-house. She did not want this known, as she imagined that people would think she hadn't money enough to go to a hotel. I may add (as every story ought to end happily) that I met Aimée afterwards, and that there was no boarding-house cloud between us.

A theatrical writer offends a great deal more frequently, unconsciously than consciously. I once knew a very clever old actress. She is alive now. She was old, and rather feeble, an entertaining and thoroughly amiable woman. One day, thinking that I could serve my newspaper and help her at the same time, I wrote a short article about her. I began it with "Old Mrs. Blank," for the simple reason that she was nearer seventy than sixty. She met a friend of mine afterwards and sent me a message.

"Tell him," she said, "never to mention my name again ; he called me 'old.' I should like to let him know that there are many older people on the stage. The idea of such a thing ! I never want any more newspaper notices. Old, indeed !"

I have since discovered that the older an actress becomes, the more intense is her desire to appear in soubrette and *ingenue* rôles. Mrs. Langtry touched upon this idea, when, in her confession, written for the London *Era*, she answered the question " How would you like to spend your old age?" with the words, "Playing *ingenues.*"

But the height of theatrical absurdity is reached when actors and actresses want to see proof sheets of the article you are writing about them. Not long ago I wrote to an actress noted for her good looks rather than for any dramatic ability, asking her for a few "points" concerning her stage life. In reply I received this:

"I am not disposed to be hypercritical, or over exacting, but so many things have been published about me which were certainly false and without foundation, in fact things having a direct tendency to injure me before the public, to whom I look for support, that some time ago I placed my affairs in the hands of able counsel. I am especially cautioned not to give my consent to the publication of any article that I do not approve. On reflection you will see how a faithful observance of said caution will protect me in the future against the appearance of any article whose tendency is injurious, and against which I have a color of procedure."

Then she went on to ask for proofs. As I was not writing an advertisement for her special benefit, but was trying to interest the public, to whom I also look for support, I could not see the whereforeness of her request, though she had, of course, a perfect right to deny me any information she did not care to give.

An actress sent me a note a couple of years ago, asking to see me concerning an article I had written about her. As it was full of well-deserved praise, I accepted the invitation with all due buoyancy. She was, however, cold and indignant.

"Do you think," she asked, "that it is quite the correct thing to allude to me as a woman? Does it not occur to you that the word 'lady' would be preferable?"

This time I indulged in a little indignation on

my own account. When I had entered her room my attention had been particularly attracted by a large family Bible that lay on one of the lower shelves of a book-case. Quick as a flash I took possession of it. It was an inspiration. I opened it at the Book of Genesis. In Chapter III., I found the following verse, which I read to her:

"And when the woman saw that the tree was good for food, and that it was pleasant to the eyes, and a tree to be desired to make one wise, she took of the fruit thereof, and did eat, and gave also unto her husband with her, and he did eat."

Then I closed the book. "The woman mentioned," I said, "was Eve, the mother of the human race. Would you sooner allude to her as the first lady and to Adam as the first gentleman?"

She laughed heartily, though at first I think she was inclined to be angry. She has never objected to any word or phrase of mine since that day. She often alludes to this little incident, and enjoys talking about it to her friends.

I have related these few anecdotes in order to show my readers that the life of the theatrical writer who is determined invariably to tell the truth and shame the devil, is not always a bewildering joy ; also, that it is much easier and frequently more felicitously resultful to gush indiscriminately over the sweet creatures of the stage. I have heard many men say, " I would sooner that those people were my friends than my enemies." Precisely. That is my case, but I don't want friends under false pretences. My books, " A Marriage below Zero," and "An Eerie He and She," were ruthlessly slaughtered by most of the literary critics. Naturally I would sooner know the men who said kind things than those who portrayed me as the villain of the age. But the evil criticisms rolled pleasantly away from me, just as water is said to slide from the back of a duck. The very worst that was said didn't cause me five minutes anguish. I weighed every criticism for what it was worth, and any points that were obviously just, I resolved to profit by in the future. Honest criticism is a boon. It is necessary for the novelist, the playwright and the actor. Injustice can always be detected. But there is far more justice than injustice in the dogmatic and literary criticisms of to-day.

Many folks wonder at the prominence given to actors and actresses. They speak sneeringly of the public interest in Miss So-and-So's private house, and Mr. This-or-That's bachelor apartments.

Say they, " Actors and actresses should be left severely to themselves when in private life. We are concerned with their dramatic work, and that is all."

I deny this entirely. Actors and actresses are a most fascinating class. By their efforts we are drawn from ourselves into a vivid world of fiction in which we live for the time being realistically. Play-going is licensed self forgetness—about the only means we have of finding that delight. No novelist, no painter, no poet can lead towards self-oblivion with any large degree of success. The theatre is the safety valve of the community. What this city would be without its play-houses, it is very difficult to imagine.

Is it at all wonderful that we want to know all that we can of the men and women whose lives are devoted to our amusement, with whom we laugh, with whom we weep, who can call forth our noblest natures, and hold our sincerest sympathies? I think not.

The newspapers feel the daily pulse of the people. They hold it throbbing in their columns. They minister to its requirements, and they minister carefully and judiciously in spite of all that is said. And the newspapers have long recognized the importance of the dramatic world. There is a great deal of trash written on the subject of sensational journalism. Suppose the American is so built that sensationalism is absolutely necessary to his welfare? I have often thought that this is the case. If the newspapers positively decline to be sensational, he will seek his food elsewhere, and very often to his detriment. A newspaper is surely justified in providing the food that is in demand. If its effect be harmful, as is the case with some news, there is the editorial as an antidote. If a people crave fascinating anecdote, and neatly told stories, you can't make them accept dry statistics and verbatim reports of the doings of Congress. Nor do I see any necessity for trying to do so. The newspaper is the mirror of the community. It reflects its good, it reflects its evil. If there be more of the evil than of the good, that is the fault of the community. The regret of the evil, the knowledge that it exists will tend more towards the remedy of the disease, than its propagation.

The desire of the public for all the dramatic news it is possible to get, is, to my mind, a sign of the healthy condition of that public. Other people may think differently. A newspaper that rigorously excludes from its columns all dramatic gossip will find its circulation in a very feeble condition. Actors and actresses are the children of the public, nourished at the breast of the public, clothed at its expense. We love to investigate them thoroughly, and we have a right to do so. Then the theatrical industry is very vast. According to the *World* almanac, there are some three thousand theatres in the United States; some five thousand actors and actresses actively employed. Hundreds of thousands of dollars are invested annually in this great plan of entertainment, this delightful education. Putting the matter practically, Americans are certainly not the people to spend their hundreds and thousands of dollars upon those with whom they are virtually unacquainted. They like their money's worth, and so do we all.

Are you not quite as interested in knowing that Henry Irving has a comfortable house in St. John's Wood, as in being informed that Queen Victoria has left London for Balmoral? Don't you think that the fact of Mme. Sarah Bernhardt's sleeping in a coffin is quite as thrilling and as useful as the intelligence that the Prince of Wales was seen walking in Pall Mall wearing a pair of tan kid gloves? Isn't a dinner given to Mr. Toole, or Mr. Wilson Barrett worth as much mention as the banquets presided over by many of the brainless "society" folks? I rather think so.

But I am getting philosophical and prosy, and without any reason. This book really didn't need a preface. Its contents deal with subjects popular, and deservedly popular with the public, and so, my kind friends, I will leave these subjects for your consideration.

ALAN DALE.

LILLIAN RUSSELL.

IMAGINE Lillian Russell, "airy, fairy, Lillian," as she is fondly called, being the daughter of the formidable Cynthia Leonard, who ran for the mayoralty of New York! Picture the velvety, cooing Lillian having for mother an advocate of woman's rights! It does seem rather incongruous, doesn't it? It is a fact all the same.

I don't believe that Miss Russell has the faintest sympathy with mamma, whose motto is rather a desperate sort of an affair for a queen of comic-opera to be expected to tolerate. But no difficulties have ever been known to exist between Miss Russell and her family, and it is said on very good authority, that the singer is a financial prop upon which many of her relatives lean rather heavily.

We are so accustomed to hear of Miss Lillian's whimsicalities and frivolities that few people know anything at all about the better side of her nature. She is one of the most kindly and most generous women in the theatrical profession. I can't help relating a couple of incidents which will substantiate what I say. These instances came under my personal attention.

While Miss Russell was at the Broadway Theatre singing in "The Queen's Mate," one of the stage hands appeared one night in a brand-new, serviceable overcoat. He hung it on a peg, and went about his usual work. Later on, it was necessary that he go out to make a purchase. When he came to the peg upon which he had hung his overcoat, he found that the garment was missing. He searched for it everywhere, but in vain. At last, in despair, the poor fellow was forced to leave without it. Miss Russell heard the story, and her heart was touched. She sent for one of the men who had seen the coat, and instructed him to go at once to a large clothier's shop, close at hand, and buy a counterpart. This was done. Miss Russell hung the coat upon the peg which had held the other. When the stage hand returned he was overwhelmed with joy to see his overcoat staring him in the face.

On another occasion one of the carpenters missed a sum of money from his purse. He had placed it there for the purpose of making a payment which was due. The loss was to him a very serious affair. It came to Miss Russell's ears during the evening. She sent for the man.

"How much have you lost?" she asked.

"Seventeen dollars," he said, the tears in his eyes. Without another word, Miss Russell drew her purse from her pocket, and handed the delighted man the sum.

Miss Russell was very indignant the other day because a few years were tacked on to her age. As a matter of fact she is under thirty, though her stage career, which began virtually at Tony Pastor's, has been so checkered, and she has been so conspicuously and continually before the public that people are inclined to make her out older than she is. This is always the way. I heard somebody say the other day, perfectly seriously, "Maggie Mitchell must be eighty, if a day." Now the fact is that she is under fifty-nine, but she came before the public at an early age, and has remained before it ever since.

Hence the many mistakes that are made on the subject of her age.

Miss Russell was married when very young to a man named Braham. She was afterwards wedded when less youthful to the ubiquitous Mr. Edward Solomon, with whom she went abroad, and encountered disasters that would frighten any prima donna. The marriage was not a very happy one.

"I had to be satisfied with one dress and a cheap bonnet," declared Miss Russell when talking on the subject, "while he had no less than sixteen suits of clothes in his wardrobe."

No wonder, under such circumstances, that there was war in the camp. Miss Lillian might have condoned infidelity, have forgiven cruelty, have forgotten deceptions, but tolerate this excess of clothes—never!

Miss Russell has a slight souvenir of "Teddy" in the shape of a charming little daughter, of whom she is alarmingly fond. Her treatment of the child is peculiar. One moment she is overwhelming it with endearments and doing her utmost to spoil the baby; at another time she is the personification of maternal dignity, correcting the youngster with the methods of an accomplished disciplinarian. Miss Lillian and her child, when in New York, live in an exquisitely furnished apartment. She has a skilled cook, a nurse, maid, and other myrmidons. Her rooms are luxurious, and well worth seeing. Miss Russell, herself, pays very little attention to dress, but she is one of the few women who can look bewilderingly beautiful even in a calico wrapper.

The little child has the most astonishing ear for music. She was able to sing from beginning to end the florid *bolero*, which was the feature of her mother's vocal efforts in "the Queen's Mate" at the Broadway Theatre. This was of course a great delight to Miss Russell, who fondly believes she has the only living example of a feminine little Lord Fauntleroy. She has recently been photographed with her little girl, and the picture is very charming. Still, it is not a good thing to circulate among the dudes and young bloods whose feeble intelligence could never imagine their lovely Lillian portrayed in what they consider the milk-and-water beauty of maternity.

Not so very long ago Miss Russell was sued by a rebellious dressmaker, and the trial was perhaps the funniest of the many funny trials I have attended. To have heard the fair Lillian's testimony, one would have imagined her the veriest pauper. She had no diamonds, no jewelry; her living expenses were really ridiculously small; her flat was the very least expensive abode she could select; her debts were very many; in reality she did not receive all her salary, her manager deducting a certain sum each week with which to efface a loan he had made her—and so on. I don't fancy that Miss Lillian's pleas of poverty impressed very many people, and I have since heard that the suit was compromised.

Of late Miss Russell seems to have settled down to business. She has now been singing at the Casino an unusually long time—for her. It must be nearly a year since she has broken a contract. She is in admirable voice, and comic opera lovers realize the fact that she is the best singer of her kind that New York has. Miss Lillian no longer appeals to dudes and young bloods. Her really excellent voice pleases the music-loving community. If only her erratic moods leave her unmolested, she still has a promising future.

Miss Russell has one great admirer of whom New Yorkers know very little. I refer to her father, Charles Leonard, the junior member of the firm of Knight and Leonard, printers, of Chicago. Mr. Leonard is a popular man, and is known around Chicago by his appreciative friends, as "Charlie."

He is extravagantly fond of his "airy, fairy" daughter, and has been known to jump on a train and travel a thousand miles, just to hear her sing. On these occasions, he always returns to Chicago immediately after the performance.

Miss Russell is invariably in a state of anxiety about her voice, and always imagining that she is losing it. She is irritable and cross when she has the slightest cold, and I am afraid that the golden dudes, who hang, in saccharine suspension, upon that lovely smile of hers, would not care to interview their goddess when she is affected by what is prosaically known as a cold. Lillian pays as much attention to her voice as does Patti, although I have never heard that she sleeps with a handkerchief around her neck, as Signor Nicolini's wife is reported to do. She has faith in cold water, as a remedy for any vocal ailment. She does not believe, like Herr Wachtel, that a glass of sweet oil is any use, neither does she credit the statement made by many of the Teutonic interpreters of Richard Wagner's "Goetterdæmmerung," that a few sips of beer are beneficial. She has heard of all sorts of remedies for vocal troubles, but does not attach any importance whatsoever to them. She says, however, that it is only by the most extraordinary care of the body that the beauties of the voice can be retained.

If Miss Russell feels that her vocal cords are in the least affected, she declines to sing. Think of this, ye unbelieving ones, who imagine that the life of a comic opera manager is one of perpetual joy, moving along on beautifully lubricated rollers. Picture the man who is at the mercy of a woman with troublesome vocal cords! Then, if you are ever disappointed by the non-appearance of your favorite prima-donna, blame her—not him.

Long journeys affect Lillian's voice. On occasions when she has to move from city to city she takes a night off, for the move, and rests most charmingly. Then, when she appears in the new town, she is as fresh and vocally delightful as ever.

There is probably no singer on the stage who cares so little for criticisms, good or bad, as does Miss Russell. They are positively without effect upon her. An adverse criticism of her voice, if well written, will make her feel that she ought to do better, and she will try to do better. But the flimsy and would-be funny paragraphs that are often hurled at her, rather maliciously, cause her amusement. She knows her own worth. Will you kindly point out to me a successful comic opera singer who doesn't? She would be a curiosity, indeed.

Miss Russell owes a great deal to her husband, "Teddy" Solomon—he of the sixteen suits. He did more for her voice than anybody she has met before or since. He saw in it a quality that with care and some little education might be made most valuable. When she went abroad with him, although they were in horrible straits, and encountered alarming misfortunes, he would never permit her to sing anywhere but in places where her vocal reputation could be enhanced. He assiduously cultivated her voice; he labored with it artistically. Much of its present delicacy and—to use the language of the Wagnerian maniacs—tone color, is due to little Mr. "Teddy's" valiant efforts. Lillian knows this. In time it will doubtless cause her to forget the horrible tragedy of the sixteen suits. She will never lose her voice if attention to its every caprice is of any avail. The most appetizing wine, the most fascinating dish will not tempt her, if she think that the indulgence will interfere with her music.

I have already spoken of Miss Russell's unostentatious charity. I must here say that she is a stern woman of business, able to drive a bargain better than ten husbands. She is thoroughly alive to her own interests, and she is quite capable of looking after herself.

I heard one of her devoted slaves, in an amorous ecstasy, remark: "Think of that brave little woman fighting her way through the world alone, unaided, forlorn."

It was too funny. I was obliged to laugh.

Miss Russell could probably retire at the present time, but she has not the least intention of so doing. She was penniless, comparatively speaking, when she returned from abroad. Since that time, the money has been flowing into her coffers in a lively stream.

I saw her the other day at the benefit given to Harry Sanderson, the manager of Tony Pastor's Theatre. She came in a carriage and sat through the performance. It was a graceful thing to do, because, as before hinted, it was Tony Pastor who brought her out. Before she came to New York, she sang in the chorus of Alice Oates' company, and of Rice's "Evangeline." Tony Pastor heard her sing, and put her on his programme—at the end of it, mind you—as an "elegant vocalist," and a "fascinating songstress." She sang ballads, and on the "list" with her was Ella Wesner, and other people of the variety stage.

That was in 1880. Tony Pastor it was who christened her Lillian Russell. His present manager, Harry Sanderson, was there at the christening. On February 7, 1881, Miss Russell sang at Tony Pastor's, the role of *Mabel* in " The Pirates of Penzance," or as it was called " The Pie Rats of Penn Yan." In the cast with her were May and Flora Irwin, William Lester, Florence Merton, John Morris and Frank Girard. Then she appeared in " Olivette," or " Oily Vet," as Tony called it. George Olmi, Dan Collyer, and May Irwin were in the cast.

It was Tony Pastor who " lent " Lillian Russell to Col. John A. McCaull, because that manager wanted her to sing in " The Snake Charmer." Mr. Pastor is very proud of Miss Russell. He feels that he had something to do with her success. I think he had. Don't you?

MRS. JAMES BROWN POTTER.

MRS. JAMES BROWN-POTTER.

A VERY diminutive edition of Mrs. Langtry is Mrs. James Brown-Potter, with none of that lady's shrewdness, none of her wonderful business capacities, and but a slight flavor of her dramatic worth. While the Langtry bursting upon a long-suffering public with little to recommend her but the pleasant notoriety conferred by the fact that she was reported to have slipped a lump of ice down the back of the Prince of Wales, bowed her head in meek humiliation to the unflattering truths of criticisms, learning the lessons that were honestly taught her with her own inimitable grace, Mrs. James

Brown-Potter emerged from the lovely insipidity of society in the full belief that she was to be a Charlotte Cushman or a Sarah Bernhardt, with drawing-room amendments.

Her career began interestingly. Nothing that will ever be written upon the manners and customs of the nineteenth century will more aptly describe their condition than the story of Mrs. Potter's appearance upon the dramatic stage. She was something of a pet in society, and clever enough, while extracting from it all the nutriment that it offered, to see its hollowness. Cora Urquhart Potter butterflied around, but she remembered each flower that supplied her with sweetness, she knew the exact measure of that sweetness. If her cleverness had been less superficial, she would not be at this time of writing wending her way to the far-off Australia, bent on conquering new fields, while those of her native land are still unvanquished as far as she is concerned.

Mrs. Potter, who is the wife of a Wall street man, of whom I have never heard a word spoken but in praise and admiration, was for some time before her appearance on the stage an amateur actress of some merit. Amateurs are as a rule so distinctly bad; their work is such a parody upon true dramatic efforts, that I am quite sure I shall be paying Mrs. Potter no supreme compliment if I declare that she was a good amateur actress. She played for charities. You know how fond society people are of "charity." If a dear young, ruby-lipped *débutante* (I use the approved word) feels that she would like her friends to see how charmingly she can enact a certain role, she always has an excuse in charity. Charity, in the world of society, is a delightful scapegoat for much that would otherwise be intolerable.

Mrs. Potter met with success as an amateur in " The Romance of a Poor Young Man." " The Old Love and the New," " Cape Mail," " A

Russian Honeymoon" and "A Moonlight Marriage." She herself boasted, not so very long ago, of the money that had been realized by the charities for which she had appeared. It was by them, however, that Mrs. Potter was able to realize her ambition. The debt is liquidated, if it ever existed.

Then came the grand *coup-d' état* in "Os'ler Joe," which so shocked sweet ingenuous Washington society. It brought Mrs. Potter more prominently before the public than anything she had previously done. It was Bismarckian. It was consummate. A cleverer stroke could never have been made. Nobody but a keen student of American foibles could have done as much.

But watch the progress of events. Mrs. Potter did not immediately announce her intention of going upon the stage. Oh no! Soon after the "Os'ler Joe" episode, discreet rumors were circulated to the effect that she probably would appear upon the boards. Her friends were mysterious; her enemies profitably venomous. Her next step was to endorse a face cream, in conjunction with Patti, Langtry and other well-known people. This was also clever. Why on earth should any woman consent to mother a printed testimonial, if she had no use for seeing her name, as it must inevitably appear? Finally, when the ground had been really most felicitously prepared, this clever, but short-sighted, lady went to Europe.

The Prince of Wales lives in Europe. If he one day abandoned his princedom in disgust, I should attribute his action to weariness of the people who live in order to advertise themselves through his medium. Kindly, unsuspecting prince! You have been of some use to humanity! You have lent the assistance of your name, ungrudgingly, to many an eager woman. You have never been tempted to deny the silly-profitable stories in circulation.

Mrs. Potter, of course, met the prince, and he

was—equally, of course—charming. Fearfully interested in her, don't you know, and all that kind of thing. Mrs. Paran Stevens, of great society pretensions, was in London, very fond of "dear Cora" and anxious to help her. Mrs. Stevens is fifty times cleverer than Mrs. Potter. With such an ally, "dear Cora" swam smoothly along the London stream. No, it was not a case of drifting. She swam. Every stroke told.

Then came her opening at the Haymarket Theatre. She herself says that she first appeared in London to gain experience. To that statement I must reply forcibly and inelegantly (please excuse me) by the simple word "bosh." Mrs. Potter knew that Anglomania raged in her own country. Her appearance at the Haymarket Theatre was calculated to give additional prestige to her New York debut.

I was present when that interesting event occurred at the Fifth Avenue Theatre. An audience of more striking brilliancy I have rarely seen; a performance of more deadly dullness I have certainly never sat through. Since that day Mrs. Potter has been a soured woman.

"I never read criticisms," has been her unvarying remark when her attention was called to the newspapers. Mrs. Potter bitterly resented every piece of advice. She had her own ideas, and used them, with a rather disastrous result. Her vaulting ambition o'erleaped itself. She was not satisfied to plod steadily towards the goal of dramatic merit. The curiosity excited by her appearance died rapidly. A fatal coldness set in. Then she made another effort and appeared in " Antony and Cleopatra," which attracted attention. What she would have done next, had she remained in America, it would be futile to try to imagine. Her American career seems to have come to an end, and she has nothing to blame but her own impulsive folly.

What a lesson the career of Mrs. Potter

teaches. What a keen satire upon society, upon the stage, and upon other equally misjudged institutions is this Potter history. If I were a cynic, I could dip my pen into gall in no better cause. But I am no cynic, my enemies notwithstanding. Mrs. Potter's intense conceit has been her bitterest foe.

On one occasion, after a "charity" performance, a friend remarked to her: "If you were to go upon the stage you would create as great a sensation as did Mrs. Langtry."

"Do you really think," asked Mrs. Potter, her eyes aglow with the fever of ambition, "that I could ever attract the attention that Mrs. Langtry has attracted?"

She excited quite as much curiosity as did Mrs. Langtry. But as I said before, she had none of the braininess of that now excellent actress. She was not bright enough to see that the curiosity she aroused was curiosity and nothing more; that with no more subtle foundation the dramatic fabric must eventually collapse in contact with criticism, as surely as does a sand castle subjected to the action of the sea. Langtry quickly fortified herself by deference to the opinions of authorities. Potter spurned them as outrageously superfluous.

Mrs. Potter never liked newspaper men, though she received them, and was always affable. She smiled at the influence of the press—too myopic to understand the mightiest mundane voice. She is superficial. Talk with her for twenty minutes and you will discover that fact, if you are an observer, though she will charm you by her bright talk and delightful manners.

Mrs. Potter is lovely. There is no denying that fact. No prettier woman could have sought the stage. But personal loveliness is not everything, though to be sure it goes a great way. It is the beautiful woman, who is frequently able to accomplish what the most daring man could never hope to succeed with. History is full of examples in substantiation of this assertion. But to her beauty must be added a mentality of no mean value.

Here is a little story concerning Mrs. Potter. Her grandmother had an unsettled claim of $40,000 against the Government for property destroyed during the war. Her mother, Mrs. Urquhart, had never been able to obtain the slightest satisfaction. Mrs. Potter decided to see what she could do. She went personally to Senator Hiscock and laid before him the merits of the case. Hiscock shortly afterwards made a speech in its favor. Friends in the Senate got the claim passed. Then Mrs. Potter called upon President Grover Cleveland and his signature was soon obtained. It was not long after this that Mrs. Potter was able to present the $40,000 to her mother.

Do you imagine that you or I, if we had devoted ten years of our lives to the endeavor, could have achieved this result? You smile at the mere idea of it. So do I. Lovely woman, my friends, is a great power, and when that lovely woman has a correspondingly beautiful intellect, the world is hers, if she wants it.

ROSE COGHLAN.

"PLEASE excuse my attire. I have only just got up, and as it is Sunday, I thought that I would just indulge in a little breakfast, *en negligé.*"

I wish you could have seen the attire that Miss Coghlan asked me to excuse. I had to bite my lip to restrain a desire to laugh. She was clad in one of the most luxurious *peignoirs* I have ever seen. It was of white and crushed strawberry (I hope I am correct) and it looked as though it might have come from Paris. Excuse her attire! I sincerely trust that she excused mine, which didn't look as though it might have come from Paris. The lovely Rose was stopping at the Hotel Marlborough, and was playing an engagement at the Fourteenth Street Theatre.

She was at breakfast, and appeared to be enjoying herself, for Miss Coghlan makes no pretense of living upon rose-leaves and dew-drops, as do many actresses whom I have had the honor of meeting.

"There is an English book," said Miss Rose, delicately dissecting an atom of—shall I tell what? Well, yes—bacon, "that gives a short account of my career—a very, very short account, because I didn't supply any data. However, I have really done a great deal of work in England, before I came to this country, that has never been chronicled. If I were to tell you everything, it would fill a volume, and you wouldn't be at all grateful."

She spoke the truth, but she wouldn't have liked me if I had assented, so I muttered one of those little "Ohs" that mean really nothing, and fidgeted in my chair to put her at her ease.

"My family wasn't at all dramatic," began Miss Rose, "until my brother Charles went upon the stage. He had been destined for a lawyer, but, in some way or other, he fell in with stage associates, and joined them. He was quite a lad when he made his first appearance. When my father died, I knew that I must do something, so my thoughts fled to Charles and the stage. He had married an actress, so he was quite theatrical."

Miss Coghlan laughed. The bacon was growing beautifully less, so there was an inducement to devote herself to her narrative.

"I appeared at Greenock, in England, when I was fourteen years old. No, sir, I will not tell you the date, and help you to add up my age. I was fourteen at the time—no matter what the time was. I played all kinds of small parts, and played them fairly well. When I was sixteen, I joined Mr. Rousby. I looked a great deal older than I was. Think of my agony when Rousby wanted me to appear as *Lady Macbeth*. *Lady Macbeth* at sixteen! 'How old do you imagine I am!' I asked, indignantly. 'Twenty-four,' was the answer. Well, they insisted upon my attempting the role, and I was so frightened that I ran away. I knew I couldn't play the part, and then I had no costumes."

Miss Rose couldn't help smiling at her youthful modesty.

"I went right up to town, which means London," she resumed, "and soon secured a position. You see, I had already gained a great deal of experience, as I had played all kinds of parts, from a singing witch in 'Macbeth,' to heavy leads. I had even appeared in the pantomimes. No, that isn't at all dreadful. In those days, a manager, when he put on a pantomime, utilized the services of each member of his company. In London, I appeared with Toole at the Gaiety Theatre. He used to play a 'first-piece' and a burlesque. Oh! I assure you that my English experience was very varied. I was liked in London, but did not make any particular hit at that time. In 1872, I first came to America. I was still in my teens."

I couldn't refrain from just a little mental calculation. The year 1872 was eighteen summers ago. Supposing that Rose were then in the last of her teens—nineteen—she would then be—

"I came to America," quickly resumed Miss Rose, "with Mr. Henderson. He was to have produced 'The Woman in White,' in this country, but for some reason or other, the scheme fell through, as theatrical schemes will do, occasionally. I was in America, so Mr. Henderson suggested that I join Lydia Thompson's company. I really made my debut in this country with that organization in 'A Happy Pair,' after playing *Jupiter* in 'Ixion' at Wallack's Theatre."

The idea of Miss Coghlan as Jupiter, "the most powerful of all the gods of the ancients," was rather funny.

"Why did I first come to America?" she went on, repeating a question of mine, "Oh, because the offer I had was a good one. I was getting £5 in England. I was offered £15 to go to America. Mr. Lester Wallack saw me the first night I appeared, and at once engaged me for his regular season. I played in the meantime with Sothern, and then went back to England to spend my vacation, intending to return to America to Lester Wallack, who had offered me $100 per week. That happened seventeen years ago."

"Eighteen years," I suggested.

"This is 1890—" in a startled tone. "Yes, eighteen years ago. Isn't that a fearful thing? Well, as I said, I went back to England, and at once got an engagement with Charles Mathews. I appeared with him as *Miss Grantham* in 'The Liar.' That was my first real comedy part. I remembered that I was shortly to return to America to Wallack. Then came an offer to play *Viola* in a big production of 'Twelfth Night,' in Manchester. I was offered £20 per week—what I was to get at Wallack's—so I promptly broke my little contract with the American manager."

Miss Coghlan said that, as though it were a matter of course that she should disregard a contract that had no longer any charms for her. And it is a matter of course with many actresses, to whom a contract means little more than the paper upon which it is written.

"'Twelfth Night' was a great success," she

said. "It ran for three months. Then I went back to London, and opened in 'East Lynne,' at the St. James'. You see my career in England, before coming here, was, as I told you, very varied. My appearance in 'East Lynne' was really my first London opportunity for good work. It brought me under the notice of the English critics. Oxenford and the others were all very kind to me. Barry Sullivan saw, and engaged me. The following season I traveled with him all over England, playing in all the big cities. It was while with him that I had offers to return to London. I accepted one and opened at the Mirror Theatre, Holborn, in a play called 'Self,' that was a dead failure. It was a lovely company, however. The people in it were charming. They next produced 'All for Her,' which ran for a year and a half."

Miss Coghlan remembered all these details. Not a note did she consult. In fact she was sitting at the breakfast table, from which the bacon had vanished.

"I told you I broke my contract with Wallack," she went on. "Well, in spite of that, he sent for me to play leading roles. I thought that by this time my experience was large enough to justify my acceptance of the position. I came to America for the second time in 1877, and have never acted out of the country since that year. I won't go all through my American experiences, for they have been published. Yes, I have made America my home. My mother is here, my brother is here, I have had a sister here, and I have a little daughter—an adopted daughter."

Miss Coghlan married a few years ago Mr. Clinton Edgerly, a good-looking young lawyer. She surprised everybody, of course, but that never does any harm in the theatrical business. Miss Coghlan has no children of her own.

"I took my little girl," she said, "when she was six weeks old, and I have kept her ever since. She is a great comfort to me. She is at present with my mother, who lives on the Western Boulevard—her grandmother, as the child says. She is a sweet little thing, and very, very bright. I also have my sister's child at the present time staying with my mother."

"Of course, your little girl will appear upon the stage?"

"If I cannot make a fortune large enough, she might do so. But the stage is not the life I should select for a girl. This perpetual traveling about is dreadful. It is a very hard life, and the temptations" (Miss Rose sank her voice) "are very great. A girl has no resources when she adopts the stage. In other days, when there were stock companies, and you could go to your theatre in August, remain there all the winter, make a home of your own, and surroundings of your own, stage life was another thing altogether. But living in railway trains, and that awful 'one night stand' system, make life something of a strain. If there were anything else that a girl could do, I would advise her to do it. The greatest blow to art and to the future of the stage, was the abolishment of stock companies."

Miss Coghlan spoke very emphatically. There is no detail connected with stage work that she cannot discuss, and discuss interestingly, too.

" How do you study your roles?" I asked.

" I go over the lines in bed," said Miss Coghlan with a smile. (I didn't blush. I thought at the time that perhaps I had better do so, but I reconsidered the matter, and came to the conclusion that there was nothing for the most prudish being to redden at.) " I repeat them over and over again. But before I touch the lines, I have made myself thoroughly conversant with their meaning, and the meaning of the play. I identify myself with the character, and I try to act it as it should reasonably be acted. Of course, every actress has, or ought to have, a personality which is better adapted to some parts than it is to others, physically and otherwise. I think some of my greatest successes have been in such plays as ' Diplomacy,' ' A Scrap of Paper,' ' Forget-me-not,' ' Masks and Faces,' ' School for Scandal,' ' London Assurance,' ' She Stoops to Conquer,' and ' Impulse.' If I had my choice, however, I would play Shakespearian comedies, and nothing else. I adore them. But it is impossible to produce them with any success nowadays. They require a very fine company, and a magnificent production. You can't cast a Shakespearian comedy at the present time. The salary list, if you wanted a good actor for every part (and to present Shakespeare properly this ought to be the case) would be simply enormous. Then actors and actresses don't like playing subordinate parts even for big salaries. They want the centre of the stage. Oh! I am very fond of Shakespearian comedy. There is some satisfaction in it. You can learn something from it.

But it is impossible, for the reason I have stated."

By this time, I thought I had stayed quite long enough. Miss Coghlan had a cold, and I felt that she ought to save up her voice for the theatre, instead of lavishing it so nobly upon me. So I said farewell, and left. As I went downstairs, I heard the waiter approach to remove the breakfast things.

"I'm not ready yet"—came from Miss Coghlan. At any rate, I reflected, I hadn't impaired her appetite. Could there still be more bacon? Oh, healthy Rose.

FANNY DAVENPORT.

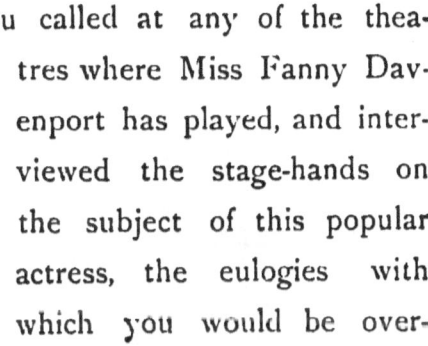

IF you called at any of the theatres where Miss Fanny Davenport has played, and interviewed the stage-hands on the subject of this popular actress, the eulogies with which you would be overwhelmed would be sufficiently voluminous to fill a good-sized book. Miss Davenport, by many little delicate acts of kindness and womanly consideration, has contrived to win the affection of all those theatrical people of whom the public see so little personally, but whose admiration is of very valuable assistance to an actor or actress.

Miss Davenport never leaves a theatre at which she has played an engagement, without depositing a cosy little sum of money for the scene-shifters, stage carpenters and other myrmidons of the theatrical manager. She has 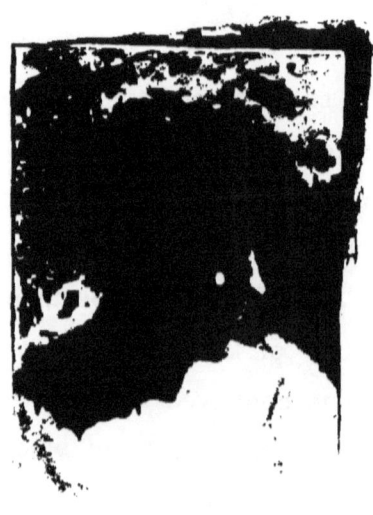 always a bright, encouraging word for everybody; she never displays any of the well-known petulance of the successful star; in a word she treats these hard-working subordinates as her friends, and the result is that they adore her, and would give her hours of their leisure time if she needed it.

"Now, boys," I heard her say on one occasion, "let me see if you can't set that scene a little differently. I think it would be better arranged so. Don't you?"

She appealed to them, as though she were thirsting for their opinion on the subject. The men had already labored diligently at that particular scene. A command from her would of course have been obeyed, but the work would have been done in a half-hearted way, and probably in a slipshod manner, too. But Miss Davenport won their hearts by this consultation. The result was that the scene was set exactly as she desired it, and each one of those men thought he was doing her a personal favor.

Miss Davenport was certainly born for the stage, if that be possible. She is the daughter of the late Edward Loomis Davenport, an actor well known to our fathers and mothers. Fanny Lily Gipsy Davenport is her name in full, though she has graciously consigned the Lily Gipsy to oblivion. She was born forty years ago in London, just opposite the British Museum, and was educated in the public schools of Boston. She is one of the few women who, successful as a child actress, has increased her popularity in womanhood.

Miss Davenport first appeared upon the stage at the Howard Athenæum in Boston, playing a child's part in "Metamora." In 1862 she was first seen in the metropolis at Niblo's Garden, the play being "Faint Heart Never Won Fair Lady." But her success begins from the time when she attracted the attention of Augustin Daly, while playing at the Arch Street Theatre in Philadelphia. The far-seeing Augustin was at once struck with Miss Davenport's possibilities, and he engaged her services. In 1869, she appeared at the Fifth Avenue Theatre under his management, and then began a long series of triumphs.

The roles in which she won fame were *Lady Gay Spanker* in "London Assurance," Dion Boucicault's still famous play, *Nancy Sykes*, in a dramatization of Charles Dickens' "Oliver Twist;" *Lady Teazle*, in "School for Scandal;"

Lu and *Fanny Ten Eyck*, in "Divorce;" *Leah*, in the play of that name; and *Mabel Renfrew*, in "Pique."

Miss Davenport discarded Augustin Daly as though he were the proverbial old glove. By him she had mounted the ladder to success. His ladder she felt she could afford to kick away. She kicked it away with considerable vigor.

She went to London and produced a play by Miss Anna Dickinson, entitled "An American Girl." She was not a great success in the English metropolis. She had become—to put it nicely—more than delicately plump; in fact too plump to play any of the parts for which she felt she was fitted.

Miss Davenport began to "bant," and so severe was the ordeal through which she voluntarily passed, that she to some extent regained her lissomeness, and is to-day of admirable proportions. Miss Davenport starved herself, and submitted to the most horrible *regime.* Only a woman of an iron will could have suffered as she suffered. It is a well-known fact that people with a tendency of *embonpoint* are very fond of the good things of this world. Miss Davenport was no exception to the rule. But she positively declined to gratify herself. She took amazingly long walks, and lived a life of torture.

She told a friend not long ago that she had ruined her health. "I never know a single moment," she said, "absolutely free from pain. I suffer all the time. I have certainly won that for which I strove, but the game was not worth the candle."

Whenever Miss Davenport hears of a young woman who is trying to reduce her "fleshiness," she sends for her, and advises her in the most emphatic terms to desist. She graphically details her own experiences, with the result that the avoirdupois-fatigued damsel comes to the conclusion that there are worse things in the world than plumpness.

Miss Davenport is at present Mrs. Melbourne D. McDowell. A few months ago she was quietly married to her leading man, though all her friends scouted the idea of her marriage, and Miss Davenport herself was understood to have indignantly denied the possibility of such an event. Just before marrying McDowell, Miss Davenport secured a divorce from Edwin H. Price, a former leading man, whom she married in 1879. He was her husband for ten years, and that isn't so bad for a prominent actress, is it?

The divorce case was tried with the utmost secrecy. Reporters scoured the city for details; every effort was made to discover the testimony. But Mr. and Mrs. Price were legally separated in the most tranquil manner. Those who say that Price interposed any objections to the divorce have no grounds upon which to base the assertion. He seems to take it in the most cheerful manner. Price is a genial, good-tempered fellow. He, this season (1890), managed a company playing "The Bells of Haslemere," but with small success. Miss Davenport is one of the best paying "stars" in the country. Her first success after she left Daly was made with Sardou's "Fedora." This she played for several seasons, and the financial results were very gratifying to her. Next came "La Tosca," from which I was told on very good authority, that last season she cleared $90,000.

Mrs. McDowell is a rich woman. She is kind-hearted and charitable. She adopted two children that were left orphaned by her sister Lilly. This lady came to America in 1854 and married Mr. Thorn. She was drowned on the yacht belonging to Mr. Garner of the New York Yacht Club. Miss Davenport cared for the two children for a long time, and finally adopted them.

But in spite of her financial prosperity, Miss Davenport is thrifty. Her company is by no means an expensive one. A short time ago, she took a day or two "off," and I understand deducted the salaries that those days would have called for, from the members of her company. There was some revolt, and one young man, at least, was dismissed. He is at present suing the fair Mrs. McDowell. He told me the other day that when he demanded his salary rather peremptorily, she posted up a notice in the green-room declaring that he had been guilty of "ungentlemanly conduct."

Actors, however, are very difficult people to manage. They are self-opiniated, stubborn and unruly, as a general rule. I cannot imagine that Mrs. McDowell would be very hard to please.

She dislikes notoriety, strange to say. Just before she produced "La Tosca," and at a time when the theatrical profession was prophesying her divorce from Mr. Price, I had occasion to write a short article on some of the difficulties of Americanizing "La Tosca." For instance, there was one scene, when she kills *Scarpia*, and then takes up a crucifix and places it at his feet, that it was thought would be indignantly received by an American audience. Miss Davenport was anxious that the scene should be given just as it was presented in France. Mr. Price wanted it omitted. It was understood that there was some little heated argument upon the subject at rehearsal. I chronicled this in due course, as a piece of "green-room gossip."

The next day Miss Davenport sent for me, and I quaked in my shoes. She assured me that the point had not been discussed; that the rehearsals had been extremely pleasant.

"You were wrong to state that Mr. Price and I had differed," she said at last. "We are in perfect accord on the question of 'La Tosca;' I should like that understood."

I comprehended. Miss Davenport was so afraid that the meaning of my article might be construed into a breach between herself and her husband, that she had been angry at it. As, however, the interest of the article concerned the play " La Tosca," and had been inspired by no idea of ruptured domesticity, I was hardly able to appreciate Miss Davenport's agony.

At this writing, she is living very placidly in a handsomely furnished flat, and taking life easily.

YOLTA.

LOTTA.

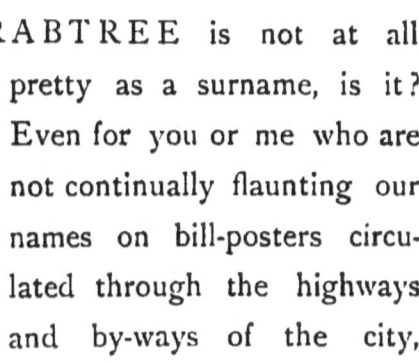

CRABTREE is not at all pretty as a surname, is it? Even for you or me who are not continually flaunting our names on bill-posters circulated through the highways and by-ways of the city, Crabtree would have but scant charm. Therefore, I say, it is hardly to be wondered at that such a dainty little lady as Miss Lotta should scornfully decline to recognize the title. There was no need to change it. Miss Lotta simply declined the assistance of any surname at all. Lotta she has always been, and Lotta she will remain to the end of her interesting chapter.

Only her enemies call her Lotta Crabtree. It sounds horrid, doesn't it?

Now, I didn't intend to say a word about the year when Lotta was born. Natal events are sometimes best forgotten, but as Mr. Augustin Daly upon the programmes of his last Shakespearian production "As You Like It," has set forth in cold type this cruel announcement,— well, I suppose I might as well face it.

Yes, the piquant little lady, who pouts and pirouettes like a veritable *enfant terrible* before the public, will, in this year of our Lord 1890, celebrate her forty-third birthday. I saw her only the other day sitting perched up childishly at the Harlem Opera House, and I wondered why it is that time frequently deals so kindly with the children of the stage, while he furrows and wrinkles us up, and plays the very deuce with our personal appearances. Yet they say that paint and powder are ruinous to the complexion. I am not at all sure of that. The old women of the stage are infinitely less time-worn than their sisters in other walks of life. Look at old Mrs. Gilbert, at Mrs. Yeamans, at Mme. Ponisi. They are far less wrinkled than women of their age who have never been behind the footlights.

But to go back to Lotta. The little lady was born in Grand street, New York, on the seventh day of November, 1847. When she was about seven years old she went to California, and at eight years of age, although such precocities as the recent little Lord Fauntleroys were unwotted of in those days, she made her first appearance in public. I believe it was as a vocalist. In 1858, she appeared as *Gertrude* in " The Loan of a Lover," in a Californian town rejoicing in the simple name of Petaluma. Lotta was first seen in New York in 1864, when she played at Niblo's saloon, making a rather unfavorable impression. Then she travelled through the west, accompanied by mamma and papa Crabtree.

It was not until 1868, after her engagement at Wallack's Theatre, that she became the celebrity she has since remained.

Everybody knows that Lotta is one of the richest women on the stage, but everybody doesn't know that she owes her cosy financial condition to the shrewd management of old Mrs. Crabtree. Mrs. Crabtree is a financier to the backbone. She has guarded Lotta's earnings with the energy of the dragon of whom we have heard in connection with St. George. The little lady has never been permitted any extravagance. In the height of her affluence, her companies have been organized with as much care and financial precision as though Miss Lotta were about to risk a barnstorming tour.

They tell me that Miss Lotta has a mortgage of $280,000 on a well-known hat factory in New York. At any rate she owns the Park Theatre in Boston, free from all encumbrances, and brother Jack manages it for her—nominally, at any rate.

Mrs. Crabtree is a terror to the actors and actresses in her daughter's company. Said a lady to me the other day: " Lotta is a dear little soul. I can get on with her admirably. But the mamma! Oh, dear me, I cannot endure her!"

Lotta is completely under mamma's control. If she were a child in the nursery she could not be more utterly mothered. In fact, it is almost absurd to see the two together, and recollect that Miss Lotta is old enough to have adult children of her own.

I called upon the little actress one day just after her return from England. She was stopping in Twenty-third street near Ninth avenue. She was attired in the most juvenile manner, in a white muslin dress, with a broad blue sash tied with infantine grace in a big bow at the back. I wanted to " interview " Miss Lotta about her season in England. But if you imagine that poor little Lotta was allowed to say very much, you know nothing whatever about dear old Mamma Crabtree. Towards the close of the interview, Lotta contrived to utter a few words. Indeed, Mrs. Crabtree, I rather imagine, began to think it best that she should do so. Lotta told me a stereotyped story about her big success, though the cable reports had related stories diametrically different.

But there has never been but one Lotta. This little lady has founded a school. Her imitators are to be counted by the thousands, and on the principle that imitation can never equal the original, Lotta still has no rival. She has encountered strong opposition from Miss Minnie Palmer, but, as an artist, Miss Palmer can no more be compared to Mrs. Crabtree's daughter than chalk can to cheese, or brass to gold. Lotta is a jealous little lady, too. Like most stars, she wants to monopolize the honors of the performance in which she appears. Her leading man must never sing too well, or act too convincingly; her leading lady must never be guilty of a personal comeliness that is too much in evidence. This is a trait that Lotta shares with nearly every star on the stage. I should astonish you were I to tell you all I know of the petty jealousies that mar the characters of those who seem to us, when on the stage, to embody all the charms that flesh is heir to.

But in private life Lotta is delightful, or as delightful as Mrs. Crabtree will permit her to be. The mamma is the daughter's shadow, ever present, ever assertive. Lotta dotes on her brother Jack, who is known as a rather wild young man, with a very good heart.

She is superstitious, like most members of the theatrical profession. I verily believe that even if danger were ahead she would stop to pick up a horse-shoe she happened to see in the street. Lotta never permits one of these symbols of luck to remain unmolested. She captures and gleefully keeps the bit of iron.

Lotta is credited with a belief in spiritualism, though I don't know that religion comes under my province. Some time ago a number of actresses wrote upon the subject to a New York newspaper, and their statements were really pathetically amusing. Mrs. Langtry declared that she never played a new part without falling upon her knees and offering up a prayer. Miss Fanny Davenport asserted that she invariably tried to follow the life of Christ, which led the witty *Truth* to remark : "Miss Davenport has kindly told us what she thinks of God, but no amount of journalistic enterprize can inform us what God thinks of Miss Davenport."

Miss Lotta has been "resting" during the present season, but she has not retired, as many people profess to have thought. Retire, with Mamma Crabtree in the field? Never!

> Lotta's not to reason why,
> Lotta's but to act or die.

And so we may 'expect to see the little lady before us until she is as old as Miss Maggie Mitchell, which will give us exactly fifteen more years in which to enjoy her performances.

HELENA MODJESKA.

AH, there is no use mentioning the subject of age. Suffice it to say, that my wife belongs to the generation that brought forth Adelina Patti, Sarah Bernhardt and Christine Nilsson."

I was enjoying a little chat with the Count Bozenta, husband of Mme. Modjeska, in their handsome suite of rooms, No. 18 West Thirty-first street. The accomplished countess was out, indulging in the feminine luxury of shopping. Her liege lord was up to his ears in ink, floundering in some "recollections" dictated by his wife. In fact, he was a beautiful picture of a marital amanuensis.

Be quite sure that I was not guilty of indelicately asking Mme. Modjeska's age. No, my friends, experience has taught me that such

questions are as unwise as they are unavailing. Every actress is induced to deal with the subject of years as did the adventuress in the comedy. This lady remarked placidly, "Let me see; I have a son twenty-eight years of age. I must, therefore, be at least twenty-nine." The Count Bozenta merely mistook my inquiries anent his wife's earlier years for a desire to learn the year of her birth.

Count Bozenta, by-the-bye, is an excellent

fellow. The husbands of actresses are always looked upon with suspicion, simply because they are the husbands of actresses. Many of them, I admit, are useless idiots. Count Bozenta is distinctly an exception. He is a man of culture and intelligence. He dotes on his Helena, and is, I am told, inclined to be jealous upon the least provocation, which is another point that is, in my opinion, in his favor.

Modjeska, at the present time, is engaged in preparing a number of magazine articles and autobiographical sketches. It is the Count who writes them, Modjeska supplying him with the notes. And he enjoys it, the good fellow. It gives him an opportunity to be useful, as Nature has denied him the privilege of being ornamental. He has a keen eye for business. I could not help laughing at his anguish when I informed him that I wanted to write just a few lines about his wife, for this book.

"Ah, my good sir!" he exclaimed, the moisture

of desperation making its appearance upon his brow, "if you make a sketch of my wife, of what use will it be that she writes autobiographies and articles? They will be of no value. I speak as a man of business."

I assured his agitated countship that I had no intention of cutting him out, and as for conflicting with the literary effusions of his better half, why, I might be a villain, but to such a depth of iniquity I was not prepared to sink without a struggle.

Mme. Modjeska herself is a delightful woman to meet. An atmosphere of refinement seems to halo her. She is daintily interesting upon any subject she chooses to discuss. The coarsenesses and trivialities of every-day life seem to be less conspicuous in her presence. She is the sort of woman you occasionally meet in novels, but less rarely in real life.

She is a consummate woman of the world; as good an actress off as on the stage. But her artificiality is not in evidence. It is to be merely suspected. I must say I like artificial people a great deal better than those brusque, good-natured creatures, who mean so fearfully well, but who offend your sense of refinement.

If you drop in to see Modjeska, and ask her for her views on the drama, she will roll you off a dear little essay on Shakespeare, whom, of course, she adores. She will tell you how it was always her ambition to interpret this great English master, and how there are no stage creations that can hold a candle to such beauteous heroines as *Juliet, Desdemona, Imogen, Isabella, Beatrice, Portia, Ophelia* and *Lady Macbeth.*

If, on the other hand, you are more earthly, and are desirous of hearing Modjeska propound her ideas—well, let us say on the subject of corsets, she will be quite ready to meet you. She will declare that she never wears such abominations, and that the lissomeness of her figure is undoubtedly due to that fact. She will show you (if you are a woman) some chamois leather substitute in which she envelops her form, and will descant on its advantages just as though she owned the patent and were trying to "push" the article.

Should you wish to pen a little article on the American girl, Modjeska will be on hand. She knows all about the American girl, and, of course, thinks her charming. (She is playing in the American girl's country, you must remember, and pocketing the dollars earned by the American girl's papa.) She will compare her with the European damsel, and make such neat little points that you will be utterly charmed, and wonder why this joy has never come to you before.

The advisability of the smoking woman, the pros and cons of early marriage, the public school system of education—Modjeska is thoroughly *au courant* with the intricacies of these subjects. She will unfold her views with such delicious volubility that even the Count will look at her in astonishment. I am quite convinced that Bozenta himself has not fully gauged the extent of his charming wife's knowledge.

Modjeska is thoroughly Americanized. She still has "estates" in Poland, but her ranch in California is more to her taste. She was born in Cracow, and was the daughter of a music-teacher named Opido. She had brothers and sisters enough to satisfy any man or woman, and she was the youngest of the bunch. There was a Simon and a Felix and a Joseph. Mr. Opido named his youngest daughter Helena on account of her Grecian head, which I think it was extremely kind of Mr. Opido to do. How many Greek heads come into the world, and, unappreciated by their parents, become known as Mary Anne, and Susan Jane. If all parents had a due respect for the prospective feelings of their offspring, there would be no more Bridgets and

Delias, and Jameses and Johnnies and Williamses. The world would be peopled by Helenas and Paulines, and Valentines and Stephanies and Marguerites.

Modjeska worked very hard as a young girl. She helped her mother to keep house. She polished the furniture, and cooked the food, and labored in the kitchen, and made herself generally useful. I wish I could add that she milked the cows. But I can't. History does not tell us whether Mr. Opido kept such articles of luxury. I may, however, say this: If there were any cows, Modjeska milked them.

She saw her first theatrical tragedy when quite a child, and of course was immediately impressed. But she did not make an appearance upon the stage until several years later. She gave her hand and heart at an early age to a young Pole named Modrzejewski. How he pronounced his name—if he ever dared to do so—I should be ashamed to try and guess.

Modjeska played for several years in her native country; then, in 1876, having married Bozenta, she visited America, going to California with the laudable intention of founding there a Polish community. This sounds very nice in theory, but I am afraid that the Polish community was not an astonishing success. At any rate, the thoughts of Modjeska tended stagewards once more, and as the Countess Bozenta, she at once appealed to a certain Mr. Harry Sargent. I have always thought that Mr. Sargent, in the wilds of California, was more dazzled by the fact that Modjeska was a real, live countess, than by any dramatic possibilities. I have omitted to say that before Mr. Sargent began to manage Mme. Modjeska she had already appeared with John McCullough.

Sargent advertised her as "Helena Modjeska, Countess Bozenta," and from that day to this, fortune has smiled upon her. Modjeska is an artist, and artists very rarely pass through the world unrecognized. I shall always believe, however, that it was the little magical word "countess" that first attracted Mr. Sargent to Mme. Modjeska, and thus hastened a reputation that must, however, have come sooner or later.

Modjeska was a great success in London, where she first appeared in "Odette." Upon her return to this country she was more popular than ever. She secured Mr. Daniel Frohman, and was by Mr. Frohman's clever methods "boomed" up to the skies. Mme. Modjeska has enjoyed the inestimable privilege of seeing managers fight for her. Only last year, Messrs. Nixon and Zimmerman, of Philadelphia, with Mr. Lawrence Barrett, were contending for her possession. Barrett won her, and this year she has been "starring" with Edwin Booth in "the Booth-Modjeska combination," as it was known.

Modjeska has one child, whose father was the gentleman with the unpronounceable name. Shall you look upon me as brutal if I mention that she is a grandmother? I hope not, for I feel it is my duty to announce to you that fact. Some few years ago her son was quietly wedded in this city at the little Polish church in Stanton street. Modjeska was there, and the details of the ceremony were given in the daily newspapers.

In my opinion, the sons and daughters of actresses ought never to be so unkind as to make their mothers grandmothers. A grandmother is a delightful institution, but managers, as a rule, don't like any but their own. Still, this relation has not affected Modjeska in the least. To be sure, she seems to have dropped *Juliet* from her repertoire, lately. But her other roles are played as charmingly and artistically as ever.

The stage cannot afford to lose Modjeska. Indeed, I hope she will be with us even when she is a great-grandmother. Art cannot age, and Modjeska is art's child.

Isabelle Urquhart.

A MOST fascinating visit was that I paid to Miss Isabelle Urquhart, of the Casino, the other day. If I were an impressionable youth, I should immediately wring from the dictionary of my mind all the gushful adjectives it contains, and lavish them unhesitatingly upon that afternoon. But I am not impressionable, and I am not a youth, and so am not tempted to "do this thing."

Miss Urquhart, at the present time, occupies a demure looking little flat overlooking the stately Metropolitan Opera House. Mamma lives with her; so does aunt, and the charming air of domesticity was enhanced by a prevailing aroma of stew on the particular afternoon of which I speak. I like a stew-y odor. There is something homelike about it. When your nostrils are preparing for a vigorous attack, headed by patchouli and musk, stew is distinctly refreshing. Miss Urquhart's flat is beautifully furnished. Arm-chairs of various degrees of comfort, tempting sofas, pictures, bamboo portieres and all the rest of it. But I noticed on the window-sill other indications of desires as domestic as the odor of stew. I saw a pocket-book that looked as though it had just been shopping, and told me that the Urquhart's soul did not rise above the bargain counter. I caught a glimpse of discarded gloves that had probably just been

removed from Miss Isabelle's tapering fingers. These little features put me at my ease, for I am bashful and retiring. I kept saying to myself, " Stew, pocket-book, gloves ; gloves, pocket-book, stew—well, she can't be very formidable."

There was the sound of an opening door behind me, and a moment later a black-clad figure stood before me.

It was the lovely Isabelle herself, swathed in a dark, diaphanous gown, freighted with scintillant beads. Miss Urquhart's face was devoid of " make-up ; " her hair was decidedly *en negligé*; and—good gracious ! how delighted. I was to recognize the fact—she had been eating that fragrant stew. She was smacking her lips, if I may use such a vulgar expression. And, after all, I reflected, why not ? Casino beauties must smack their lips occasionally just like other people.

"Yes, I am very domesticated," said the Urquhart, making herself at home, and inviting me to do likewise. "We enjoy ourselves in this little flat, I assure you. But I don't like it. I pine for a house. I yearn for stairs. I mope for want of exercise. As there is an elevator here, of course I always take it. But I really must have stairs, soon. I can't do without them."

The picture of the stately, Juno-esque Urquhart frantically running up and down-stairs was an extremely edifying one to me. I couldn't help smiling. She saw this, and sympathetically assisted me by smiling also. Then, if there had been any ice at all between us, it was instantly broken, and Miss Isabelle chatted in a sort of Tennysonian brook-like way about herself and her career.

"I have not been before the public so very long," she said, as if apologetically, "for before 1881, I had never been upon the stage. I had sung in choirs in the convent where I was educated."

Urquhart in a convent! I felt inclined to say, " Prince ! This is too much !" but I bit my lips and looked as meek and stupidly uninteresting as usual.

" In 1881," she went on, " I sang at the Standard Theatre in ' Billee Taylor.' The house was then under the management of the late William Henderson. I had not a very large voice, and I have not improved in that direction I am quite sure " (very modestly) " but I think I did the best I could with the scanty material at my disposal. Then I was seen for three consecutive evenings in an opera called ' Elfins and Mermaids.' Ha! Ha! It makes me laugh when I remember that production. It was called ' a serio-comic opera in two acts by Charles Brown.' I was getting twelve dollars per week, but I was happy, until I heard that the manager had run off with the money, after he had given three performances. Then I felt just a trifle less elated, as you may imagine. After ' Elfins and Mermaids' I sang a very small part in a comic opera called 'Claude Duval,' in which D'Oyly Carte was interested, and then, for the time being, my connection with comic opera came to an end."

Miss Urquhart puzzled charmingly for a few minutes. Then she resumed: "Next I went to Daly's Theatre, and appeared in the legitimate. That is where I ought to be this minute, if, indeed, I ought to be anywhere on the stage."

I interrupted, as I was bound to do, and murmured: "Indeed you ought!" When I come to think of it, my words were somewhat vague in their meaning. But Miss Urquhart evidently understood my good intentions, for she went on:

"I played in 'The Passing Regiment,' 'Odette,' 'Needles and Pins,' and an old woman of ninety-seven in 'The Squire.' I was seventeen at the time, so I am not quite sure that I relished appearing as a nonogenarian. I played the role, however. Why did I leave the comic-opera stage? Because, my dear sir, I wanted to act.

I was always possessed with the idea of being a *Lady Macbeth*. I thought a position at Daly's would be a splendid thing for me, so I jumped at his offer. If I had stayed there, I should have amounted to more than I do now."

She paused and I said something pretty and consoling. I love the task of comforting people.

"I went back to the comic opera stage for mercenary motives. You are better paid there. In the legitimate you have to work for years for a reputation. A man named Harry Pitt told me that Daly would never do anything for me, and, unfortunately for me, I believed all he said. Before returning to the comic opera stage I went with this Mr. Pitt's comedy company, and played in 'Forgiven' and 'The Two Roses.' The enterprize was not at all successful. Upon my return to the Standard Theatre I sang in 'The Merry Duchess' with dear Selina Delaro. After that, I made a début in burlesque in 'Orpheus and Eurydice,' and later, succeeded Pauline Hall in the role of *Mars* in 'Ixion.' Am I wearying you?"

Wearying me? Ha! Ha! Ha! As though I could be wearied by this silver chatter, studded occasionally with jewels of wit. I said all this, in less stilted language.

"I first went to the Casino when Lillian Russell returned from Europe. I sang with her in 'Polly;' after that I returned to my beloved 'legitimate,' and appeared with Lawrence Barrett in Shakespearian plays. I was *Portia* in 'Julius Cæsar;' *Gertrude* in 'Hamlet' and *Hero* in 'Much Ado about Nothing.' But all the time I was with Barrett, I was studying singing. I had come to the conclusion that opera was my forte. I got a night off, and appeared at a concert with my professor's pupils. I suppose it was because the pupils were all so bad that I appeared to advantage. At any rate I made a hit, sang subsequently at a number of benefits, then joined the Casino company, with which I have remained ever since."

Miss Urquhart had certainly given me an imposing array of facts. Her own little reflections came afterwards.

"I prefer legitimate drama to comic opera," she said. "I would give anything in the world if I could be successful with it, and never, never appear in a comic opera again."

Oh! cruel Urquhart! Oh! pitiful "dudes!" Oh! forlorn, wretched baldheads!

"Comic opera is so very unsatisfactory," she said. "People go to comic opera simply to see pretty, bright young women."

"Well?" I dared to interrupt, trying to make eyes.

"Oh, I am bright enough, and all that," she said, "but how long will it last, and what is to become of me when it is over? Pretty girls are always springing up, and crowding out those who have been for any length of time before the public. If you outstay your time, people say, 'Why, I remember her twenty years ago; she must be ninety!' It is really sad. I am so much in love with the stage, that I don't want my career to come to an end just as soon as any good looks I may possess happen to leave me. I am passionately fond of the stage. I like it better to-day than I did when I first tried it. Don't imagine that I am finding fault with the Casino. I am charmingly treated there. I am merely dissatisfied because I can't help picturing a time when I shall have out-lived my comic opera usefulness, and be unable to do anything else. Even if I were very, very rich—which I am not—I would still act. If I go to the theatre and see a good play, I can't enjoy it, because I always say to myself, 'Well, why am I not in it?' An awful condition of things, is it not?"

Miss Urquhart showed me albums filled with photographs of herself, in all costumes. She possesses a picture of herself in that very slight attire which, a few months ago, caused so many unflattering remarks to appear in the newspapers.

"I was miserable," said Miss Urquhart, "and my appearance in that awful dress was not through my own fault, either. When I saw it, I went to the stage manager, and begged him not to let me wear it. I knew it would create an uproar. I was beside myself with anxiety. 'Miss Urquhart,' said he, 'I am directing this production. You are under my direction. You must wear that dress.' So I wore it, and one wretch in a weekly paper declared that my—my—legs looked as if they would support anything from the Equitable building to the Brooklyn Bridge. And so they did. It was the effect of the top boots, which consumed yards and yards of patent leather. It was a most trying experience for me. Now, however, I design all my own clothes, and have them made. I get extra money for this, and it is far more agreeable for me."

An awful idea that the fragrant stew I have before mentioned might by this time be cold, and that Miss Isabelle might need a little more before consigning it to the oblivion of the larder, caused me to seize my hat with sudden resolution. Miss Urquhart said very many pleasant things, and I tried to say as many more. In fact we kept up this little game of complimentry battledore and shuttlecock until I found myself locked in the elevator, en route for the street. Yes, that visit to Miss Isabelle Urquhart was certainly very fascinating.

SADIE MARTINOT.

DEAR little, bubblesome Sadie! I feel that I am not in the least disrespectful in thus alluding to Miss Martinot. I knew her before she was stately; before she could address her French maid in irreproachable French; before her pictures were in very great demand. Under the circumstances, nobody will deny me the right to exclaim, and even to repeat: Dear little, bubblesome Sadie!

Miss Martinot is an excellent example of how a bright, pretty woman can push her way rapidly to the front in the theatrical profession. Miss Sadie is of lowly origin, though history is rather dead upon the subject. I believe she was discovered in Boston by Fred Stinson, a young theatrical man. He was attracted by her charming face, dulcet voice and dainty manner. He married her.  For some time Miss Sadie Martinot was Mrs. Fred Stinson. Now the Sadie could be a prima donna if her desires ran in that direction, while Stinson is pegging away at management, his latest scheme in that direction being aimed at Miss Mary Shaw.

Miss Sadie Martinot was originally—and I say it in no perverse mood, for to my mind, it is no grave fault—Sarah Martin. She became Martinot when she went upon the stage. She is still

Martinot. Numbers of comely young women whom I could name, would not in the least mind being Martinot. The young woman was born in 1861. She is so pretty that if I were to name 1871 as her natal year, you would feel no inclination at all to dispute my statement. But I am in love with the truth, and the truth it shall be.

I first met Sadie in 1883 in London. She was then playing at the Comedy Theatre in Panton street, in the opera of "Rip Van Winkle." Miss Martinot was the *Katrina;* Miss Violet Cameron was singing the leading feminine role.

Sadie was a very meek, unpretentious little lady in those days. She got £20 a week and thought herself lucky. She was the protégée of Dion Boucicault, and that keen discoverer of talent saw the bright possibilities of the little Martinot girl. When she left the London fogs, for New York sunshine,—and she hated London with true American consistency—she appeared in New York in a series of Dion Boucicault's plays, meeting with considerable success. Later, she was seen in "Confusion," at the Fifth Avenue Theatre.

I saw Sadie some years after, and how time had changed her! She had just returned from a home that she had furnished in Vienna. She had left the stage for some time, and had been living abroad. Her return to this country was made in order that she might assume the title role in "Nadjy," at the Casino, where she had made a great hit in "Nanon."

Sadie was inclined to put on what is called "frills." She was stopping at the Vendome Hotel, and she received me in a magnificent suite of rooms. Her attire was regardless of expense. She was swathed in a white gauze *peignoir*, with furbelows up to her eyes. It was negligently open at the corsage, for Sadie has a neck and throat that half the society women in New York would give ten years of their lives to possess. Mamma was there. Mamma is a very discreet individual, who wears black alpaca and talks in a neutral tone.

"I was quite a success, was I not, mamma?" asks Sadie.

And mamma says, "Yes, dear."

"I had no intention of doing such and such a thing, had I, mamma?" pouts Sadie.

And mamma says, "No, dear."

This is merely to give you an idea of how useful a stage mamma is on certain occasions. Mrs. Martinot is generally in the vicinity of her pretty daughter, but sometimes she stays at home while Sadie goes abroad.

Well, Miss Martinot never appeared in " Nadjy." Miss Jansen filled her place. Though Sadie bought costumes and made all imaginable preparations, she declined to submit to the arbitrary stage management at the Casino, and resigned. Her indignation when she told me of this was amusing enough to have brought smiles to the face of the weeping philosopher, Heraclitus.

"The idea!" she exclaimed. "I am an artist, and do not care to be instructed in details. I went to great pains abroad to see how the part was to be played, and I could have made it extremely interesting. But to have mere details insisted upon—well, I would not submit to it. So I resigned, and one of these days I hope to have another opportunity at the Casino. I am on the best of terms with Mr. Aronson, am I not, mamma?"

And mamma said, "Yes, dear."

Miss Martinot created a sensation when she appeared at Amberg's Theatre last season. For the plucky little lady had mastered the German language sufficiently to be able to sing the leading role of *Bettina* in "The Mascot," with Mr. Amberg's German company.

Oh! wily Amberg! How well he knew that the presence of the Martinot would fill his house with the dudes and the *jeunesse dorée* of New York as it had never been filled before, and will, in all likelihood, never be filled again. Sadie made a delicious little Teuton. Her accent was simply enviably good, and though Sadie's *chic* is considerably greater than her voice, her effort was distinctly creditable.

Miss Martinot is at great demand at benefits when pretty girls are required to sell bouquets and cajole good men into purchasing them. And nobody can do this better than Sadie. A well-known man about town went on one occasion to a certain theatre, where an important benefit performance was being given. Sadie was selling flowers in the lobby. She was bewilderingly beautiful and she knew it—*petite coquine!*

The gentleman looked at the buds and looked at Sadie. She was the fairest flower of the bouquet. He picked up one of the blossoms, the intrinsic value of which was perhaps two cents. But he felt very magnanimous as he glanced at the comely seller.

"I'll get a smile from her at any rate," he mentally resolved.

Fumbling in his pocket he drew forth a five-dollar bill, and put it down in front of the charming Martinot. There was no smile upon her face. There was even a little expression of pique hovering around her red lips.

"Only five dollars!" she exclaimed with a sigh. "Why, that is the very smallest sum that has been offered this afternoon, and all the other girls have got better prices."

It was a picturesque little bit of fiction, but it was wildly successful. The gentleman took from his pocket a bill. He looked at it. Then he frowned. It was worth $20. He had no change. Miss Sadie saw his perplexity, and in a moment one of the most luscious smiles that he had ever seen was all his. She even spoke to him, in rippling mirth. Of course he was only human, and he was instantly overcome. His bud had cost him $25.

At the present time Miss Martinot is doing nothing, theatrically. That is her own fault. She is generally in demand.

Georgia Cayvan.

I HAD never met Miss Georgia Cayvan until I called upon her in her dressing-room at the Lyceum Theatre the other day. But I had criticised her performances, and it occurred to me with horrible force, as I waited at the stage door to be admitted into her presence, that I had once called her "precise and podgy." I became seriously frightened. Who could tell what she might not do to avenge herself? Suppose she locked the door of the dressing-room as soon as I entered, and stabbed me with a pair of scissors or a penknife. It would be an advertisement for her, but it might be a serious inconvenience, or more, to me. I thought it all over. I felt that the jury would acquit Cayvan, and saw that she might even be "starred" on the strength of her exploit.

"Miss Cayvan will see you in five minutes."

I heard the voice at my elbow, and turning, saw a meek little woman with fair hair. She wore an apron, and looked very subdued. In my anguish, I at once jumped to the conclusion that Georgia was utilizing the five minutes in sharpening her penknife, or putting a keener point to her scissors. I felt that I was "in for it." I could now only await events.

The five minutes passed all too quickly. At their expiration, the fair-haired girl in the apron appeared again, and beckoning to me to follow her, led the way into the dressing-room of the talented Georgia. Miss Cayvan was attired in the sumptuous ball dress worn in the second act of " The Charity Ball." She looked charming. Her bodice, cut low, showed a neck that was a revelation. How could I have called her "podgy?" Her arms glistened in their rounded sleekness, while her large brown eyes seemed to look me through and through. She was so polite that all my fears vanished. There were no scissors in sight to disturb the equilibrium that I had nearly secured.

"I am very glad indeed to see you," said Miss Cayvan (perhaps she hadn't read the "podgy" paragraph) "and I hope you will excuse the disorder of this room."

I glanced around the apartment. It was as pretty a little place as an actress could ask for. It was about the size of a band box; lighted by electricity, and draped everywhere with pale blue cretonne. There were looking-glasses, a nice comfortable sofa, a wardrobe from which glimpses of silks and plushes could be obtained, and a dressing-table covered with the appliances of stage "make-up."

I can't say that I felt at home. It would be absurd to pretend that I was completely at my ease in this dressing-room, with the gorgeous Cayvan eyeing me half suspiciously, and the fair-haired girl—who was none other than Miss Alice Cayvan, Georgia's sister—passing and repassing, in a fit of tidiness.

I asked Miss Cayvan to tell me all she could about herself, and sat down to listen to her.

"You *are* Mr. Alan Dale?" she asked, half incredulously.

"Surely."

I was not surprised at Georgia's query. I was a little bit flattered—at my own expense. I saw that she found it difficult to believe that the stupid looking creature in the black overcoat could have a single idea of his own. As I said before somewhere, I have come to the conclusion that I look a fool. Georgia's question was additional confirmation.

"My family was not a bit dramatic," began Georgia, presently. "I believe that my eldest sister played twice in private theatricals, but if I have ever done anything for the theatre" (with cast down eyes) "it wasn't because I inherited any tendency in that direction. I was born in Maine, but we moved to Boston when I was a very little child. My mother says that when I was three years old, I held a candle at a church entertainment, wore a nice little white nightgown, and had to say 'good-night.' I made a great hit."

Miss Cayvan looked at Alice, as though expecting her to say something, but the sister was hard at work arranging Miss Georgia's costumes.

"Later," said Miss Cayvan, "we met with

reverses, and I felt that I had to do something to help my family. So I resolved to be a reader, and soon found that the occupation was enjoyable and profitable. I supported myself entirely in this way, and even paid for my own schooling. It was very delightful. I met charming people, and made a good deal of money. Even now, I often come across men and women I knew in those days. I made some splendid friends. The associations of the life of a reader are excellent. I had told my mother, when I was five years old—so she says—that I meant to go upon the stage, but I forgot that until, at one of my readings, I met Steele Mackaye. He told me that if he ever had a theatre he would like to have me in it. Of course that put the idea into my head once more, but I did not appear until 1880, when I made my début at the Madison Square Theatre."

"In 1880?"

"Certainly," laughed Miss Cayvan. "I seem

to have been millions of years before the public, don't I? Now confess that you thought I first appeared in 1820, and that I am just reaching my ninetieth year? You won't confess? Very well. I went upon the stage against the advice of everybody on earth. They all had something to say against it. I remember I promised I would buy my mother a pair of lovely horses, but I haven't done so yet."

Miss Cayvan sighed, but it was not a mournful sigh. She wasn't foolish enough to pretend that she wasn't satisfied with herself. She has done great things. In ten years she has gained the position of leading lady in one of the best stock-companies in the American metropolis.

"Since I have been on the stage," she said, "I have appeared in hardly any plays that have not had long runs. I don't like that at all. I find that long runs narrow one terribly. It has narrowed me. I used to think when I was reading that the stage would be delightful for the simple reason that an actress had to appear in but one character each evening, while in reading she had to impersonate several. But now I see that I like plenty of variety, I don't get it. I appear in plays that run for two hundred nights. That is one of the penalties you must pay for a successful manager. A long run is a boon to him. He pockets his profits and has nothing to think about. We, poor things, have to go on stagnating. I would play anything for the sake of variety. I'd even be *Topsy*, for a change."

My imagination could not stretch to the point of picturing the gorgeously attired woman before me, with a black face, exclaiming, " I 'spect I growed," with the *Topsy* accent.

" Of course, before I went upon the stage, I wanted to be tragic," she resumed, " but I don't mind now what I play, though I feel I am very bad in comedy. I generally play emotional parts. I suppose you think I am very phlegmatic and placid?"

The horrible belief that she was going to say "podgy," when she began to utter the word "placid" struck me. I grew crimson in the face, and I am now firmly convinced that she knew the reason for this. I answered hesitatingly that I had been slightly inclined to the belief that she was phlegmatic and placid.

"That's what everybody thinks," she said, rather scornfully. "Well, I am not. I am fearfully nervous, and am always under treatment for my nerves."

I looked at the smooth white throat revealed by the low cut bodice; I glanced at the plump arms, and the full face. No, Georgia hadn't converted me.

"I suffer fearfully from stage fright," she continued, "and am really pitifully shaky on a first-night. If you ever saw me at rehearsal, and were manager of the company, you would discharge me. I do the most awful things. I really behave more like a cow than anything else."

This was getting embarrassing. What could I say?

"Fortunately, Belasco, our stage manager, knows me. We had a dress-rehearsal of the 'Charity Ball.' There was nobody in the house but one or two of the Lyceum directors, whom I knew, but I was so frightened that I couldn't do anything. Do I feel the parts I play? Oh, Alice, he asks me if I feel the parts I play."

Miss Cayvan cast a look of withering contempt upon me, and turned to her sister. Miss Alice Cayvan was not a clever confederate. She didn't seem to know what to say. So she said nothing, and left Georgia to fight her own battles.

"Do I feel the parts I play?" repeated Miss Cayvan, in accents of sorrow. "Do I feel the parts I play? You may not like my acting, but surely—well, I will simply say that I have terrible weeping fits; that for days and days I don't eat; I don't sleep; and I subsist entirely upon beef tea."

Again I looked at the smooth white throat revealed by the low cut bodice; I glanced at the plump arms, and the full face. No, Georgia hadn't converted me.

"I never learn a line of a part until I thoroughly know what it is all about," she said. "I never study a part until I have acquired every bit of the dramatic action. The lines come later on. I find that when I have completely mastered the meaning of a part, the lines are learned very easily. I know other people do differently, but I can't help thinking that my method is the best. I do all I can to improve myself, mentally. An educated person can do much more upon the stage than an uneducated one. I always have a book with me on the cars, and I attend lectures—and so on. People laugh at Boston girls, and call them bluestockings, but I assure you that a Boston training is a great thing—and a great help for the stage, too. I think that my reading experience assisted me a considerably."

Miss Cayvan had very little to say on the associations of the stage. "My experience has been an exceptional one," she remarked. "You see I began at the Madison Square Theatre, and have been mostly in New York companies, which are like large families. Here, at the Lyceum Theatre, I feel as though I were at home. Of course, for sixteen weeks I 'barnstormed.' I then had an opportunity of seeing what the associations of the stage *might* be. An actor's nature is peculiar. He is essentially different to other men. He is placed in queer surroundings, and, of course, he is affected by them. No matter how hard you try, you have the flavor of the stage hovering around you. I suppose I have some of it, myself."

"Have you reached your theatrical goal?" I asked.

"I don't know," she said. "I have not realized my dreams. There is a saying that if you are true to your dreams, they will be realized. I suppose that I have not been true to mine. But of course my position is a very comfortable one," (briskly). "Here I am in an excellent company, passing myself off as leading lady" (laughing). "I suppose I couldn't be a star. Starring isn't dignified, anyway. A star requires great notoriety, great beauty," (with a glance at the mirror) "or some mental exaltation that leads her to believe she is greater than anybody else. Some people are fitted for stock companies and for nothing else. I believe that I am one of those people."

At that moment Miss Cayvan was called to the stage. "My order of dancing, please, Alice," she said as she picked up her train and made for the door. The little programme was handed to her by her sister, and with a bright smile she took her departure. Alice didn't look at all encouraging, so I decided to follow suit.

After all Georgia hadn't been so terrible.

Copyright 1887, by NAPOLEON SARONY.

MRS. LANGTRY.

Mrs. Langtry.

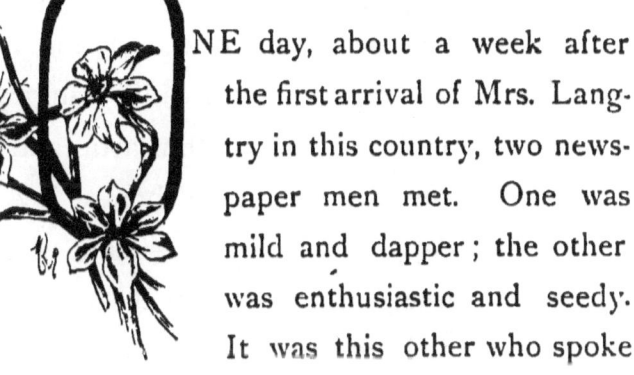

ONE day, about a week after the first arrival of Mrs. Langtry in this country, two newspaper men met. One was mild and dapper; the other was enthusiastic and seedy. It was this other who spoke first in a genial burst of confidence.

"George," he said, "you know I interviewed Mrs. Langtry the other night. I'm an old hand at that sort of thing, old fellow, as you are aware, but confound it, if I didn't succumb to her." And, sinking his voice to a whisper, "I think I must have made an impression, for she gave me this."

He held up a portrait of the beauteous Langtry. On its back was inscribed this legend: "With sincere regards, from Lillie Langtry."

The sallow face of the enthusiastic and seedy young man flushed with an elaborate joy. The mild and dapper youth was silent. Then he carefully drew from his pocket an envelope, opened it, and produced another portrait of Mrs. Langtry, exactly similar to the first, and bearing the same bland and interesting legend.

"She gave me this," he said. It was a sad blow to the seedy enthusiast. He began to realize that all that glittered was not necessarily gold, and without a word went his way.

This little anecdote, which has the merit of truth, is illustrative of Mrs. Langtry's character. Of gentle birth, and accustomed to mix in most exclusive and ultra-cultivated circles, she brought to her theatrical surroundings all the delicacies of refinement. In reality the newspaper men she met were simply treated as a well-bred hostess would treat guests. But so unusual was this method to the frequently insulted interviewers, that each imagined himself to be an especial object of her favor.

Mrs. Langtry won a great deal of her success in America by the newspapers. Like the Hon. Chauncey M. Depew, she made it a point to be particularly and effusively kind to the gentlemen of the press; to answer all their questions and to receive them as friends. It is generally admitted, in Mr. Depew's case, that to this policy is largely due his almost universal popularity. And it has also been the case with Mrs. Langtry. It has been said that the most influential figure on a newspaper is the reporter. While I do not admit this very entirely, I assert that the statement contains many grains of truth.

Let me give you an instance of Mrs. Langtry's delicacy. With half a dozen other newspaper men, I once called at her house in West Twenty-third street, after her arrival from England.

The house, which was the property of Mrs. Beach Grant, mother of Miss Adèle Grant, had been taken, in its exquisitely furnished condition, by Mrs. Langtry. It stands back from the street, and pedestrians still look at it, as they " pass by."

We were admitted by an admirable specimen of the English flunky, with a delightfully stolid look of know-nothing-ism written upon his features. He showed us into a reception-room that was simply a feast for the eye. Tapestry hung upon the walls, the portières were of yellow silk, the carpets of the thickest velvet, and in all directions were quaint little tables loaded with daintiest bric-à-brac, and "articles of virtue," as Mrs. Partington would say.

Mrs. Langtry frou-froued into the room in a few moments, and before we were aware of it we were at home. A more charming hostess was surely never revealed. It is a melancholy fact that a number of misguided people suppose that the American newspaper-man is not completely at his case until he is at the flowing bowl. A more gross calumny has never been imagined. Perhaps years ago, when the country was young, and any Tom, Dick, or Harry who could sign his name was permitted to write for the daily journals, this may have been the case. At the present time, the journalists of the metropolis are, for the most part, gentlemen by birth and education.

Well, I suppose Mrs. Langtry had been told what she ought to do under the circumstances— to offer wine. This lady, however—I use the term advisedly—did the thing in her own graceful manner. This is how she managed it. She rang the bell. James, the know-nothing-istic flunky appeared.

"I am dying with thirst," she said to him, "and after my journey, I *must* have a glass of champagne. Please bring me a bottle, James. Don't think this awful of me," she added, turning to us, "but I am truly fatigued, and if you are charitable, and want to put me at my ease, you will join me."

Could anything be more tactful or delicious? I, who had registered a vow never to "quaff" with actors or actresses was disarmed. So was everybody else. We had a most enjoyable visit, and, be quite sure that the Langtry had made no enemies.

I have met Mrs. Langtry a score of times at her house and at the theatre. On every occasion I have found her the same. Of course she is a clever woman. She calculates upon the effect of everything she does, but in an artistically imperceptible manner.

To her subordinates Mrs. Langtry is always the quintessence of politeness. That flunky of hers adores the ground she walks upon. Although she is now in England, and he is in the city in the service of her boon companion, Mrs. Baron Blanc, I am convinced that, at one word from Langtry, he would meet her, were it at the farthest end of the earth.

A friend of mine, a newspaper man, who had been asked to write up a series of articles upon Mrs. Langtry's *menage*, had occasion, of course, to visit her very often. One winter day he slipped upon the icy pavement, broke his leg, and was taken, helpless, to the hospital. Mrs. Langtry heard of this, and every day for the following month her carriage was to be seen at the hospital. She visited the sick man, took him fruit and flowers, and did it all in such an irresistibly fascinating manner, that if to-day the object of these attentions were called upon to offer himself up for her, I am quite sure that he would not hesitate.

There was a funny side to this episode. The young man in question was engaged to be married to a pretty girl who lived exactly opposite Mrs. Langtry in Twenty-third street. She, of course, saw her *fiance* visiting the actress, and made things so "hot" for him that he finally discontinued these visits.

Mrs. Langtry used to give artistic little dinners at her Twenty-third street house every Sunday night when she was in the city. Her mother, Mrs. Le Breton, and her little niece were generally living with her. Her guests generally included Mrs. Baron Blanc, Mr. Frederick Gebhardt and Mr. Porter Asche, not necessarily at the same time.

Of Mrs. Langtry, as an artist, I shall say but little, for has not this been spoken of in the daily journals since her first appearance in 1883? She has vastly improved. Her *Lady Ormond* in " A Wife's Peril " is a distinctly creditable piece of work, and the conscientious efforts of the keen-witted woman to rise above the mere level of a professional beauty have been extremely visible.

It was a great blow to her when Mrs. Potter produced " Antony and Cleopatra." She had intended to do this herself. Still she was not completely daunted. In her intense desire to win dramatic fame, she appeared at the Fifth Avenue

Theatre last season as *Lady Macbeth.* Everybody accorded her performance the highest praise. She was a revelation.

Poor Langtry! The public declined to patronize her in this—for her—novel role. They wanted her Worth-arrayed, jewel-bedecked, a drawing-room doll. "Macbeth" was a financial failure, and Langtry went to Europe. At this writing she is "touring" the English provinces. She will undoubtedly return to this country, to which she owes her success. Mrs. Langtry is a rich woman. She owns a great deal of American real estate, and has a lawyer on this side of the Atlantic who looks after her many interests. She, herself, is a consummate woman of business, and what she doesn't know about America and American modes of life—well, it is of no consequence to anybody.

MARY ANDERSON.

THE Our-Mary-ness of Miss Anderson is fast wearing away. It is being gradually replaced by a Their-Maryness that may enhance her value in the eyes of Anglomaniacs, but which, to true Americans must be rather galling. To be sure, art is universal. Still, men and women like to remember that the artist is bound to them by that poetic tie of nationality, which no naturalization papers on earth can ever really sever.

Mary Anderson, the American girl, now resides in England. The land which gave her birth, the country in which she made her first success, is hardly good enough for the dainty lady to live in. She makes periodical visits in the approved style, with an English company, and then goes back to London to spend there the good dollars she has earned. During her visit in 1889, the Westerners attacked her rather savagely, and poor Mary, not understanding that rabid patriotism was unconsciously at the root of the attack, was very much hurt.

In fact, many people consider that the severe and unjustifiable treatment she received in St. Louis was the cause of that "nervous prostration" that rendered her unable to carry out her season's engagement. She went back to England to recuperate in its finer atmosphere. Interviewers on this side of the water were treated with rigid contempt. Miss Anderson declined to explain herself. But no sooner was she upon the shores of Albion than she indulged in the unbosoming process. It was the difference in the air, I suppose, that rendered this possible.

I remember the occasion of Miss Anderson's return to this country, after her first success in London. The susceptible hearts of all New York's interviewers fluttered bewilderingly at the delightful prospect afforded them by an Anderson interview. The arrival of the steamship that brought her here was eagerly awaited. Columns of the most interesting gossip were confidently expected.

The morning following her arrival, however, showed clearly the vanity of human wishes. Meek little paragraphs appeared in the morning papers announcing Mary's advent, and giving, third-personly, the details of her plans. The only paper that published an interview, such as it was, was the *Tribune;* such a wretched, rambling, disconnected affair, too! And can you guess how it was obtained? Why, the interviewer managed to get on board the vessel at Quarantine, and listen to stray remarks that fell from Mary's lips, as she conversed with a companion. Of these he attempted to make a "talk." Miss Anderson positively declined to be interviewed. It wasn't English. It wasn't dignified. If ever a disgusted set of men existed in New York, it was the set whose hopes had been dashed to the ground by the Anderson.

Contrasted with this superlative exclusiveness is the story told me by a gentleman who lived in Louisville and knew Mary when she was a young girl.

Said he, "Why, I have seen her mount the wash-tubs and recite from 'Romeo and Juliet' with a wealth of gesticulation that was astonishing. Her audience was a colored washerwoman and cook. They were amazed at her performance, and used to applaud it vigorously. Her arrival in the kitchen was a signal for the cessation of all work. Juliet on the tubs was quite an institution."

Mary Anderson is not a Louisville girl, as many people suppose. She was born in Sacramento, California, in 1859, but her parents moved to Kentucky when she was very young. She went to school in Louisville, but rebelled at the routine work of the institution. In fact, Mary's love for the stage really seems to have begun very young, and to have been sincere and worthy. She studied Shakespeare with earnestness, and was perpetually poring over the works of the great dramatist.

J. M. Farren tells us that she paid a visit to Charlotte Cushman on one occasion. The old actress took Mary's hand, and patted her affectionately on the cheek. "You have three essential qualifications for the stage," she is reported to have said, "voice, personality and gesture. With a year's longer study and some training, you may venture to make an appearance before the public."

Mary first made this venture in Louisville, at Macauley's Theatre, in 1875, in the character of *Juliet*, a role for which she is absolutely unfitted, which she has played many times since, and which she may continue to play for years to come, without even realizing Shakespeare's meaning. The idea of Mary Anderson playing *Juliet* has always seemed to me grotesque. Sarah Bernhardt in one of Charles H. Hoyt's farce-comedies would not be more misplaced.

In 1877 she was first seen in New York, and since that day has always been able to "draw" large audiences in this city. It is Miss Anderson's beauty rather than her talent that first attracted attention. Her dramatic worth has always been questioned until she appeared in

"A Winter's Tale;" her beauty nobody has ever attempted to deny.

I do not believe that any woman has been photographed as persistently as has Miss Anderson. Her pictures have literally adorned the city's highways and by-ways. And it has been the same in London. Her personal charms won instant recognition.

Miss Anderson's work in "A Winter's Tale," in 1889, was really the first dramatic effort she has made that met with general approval. As *Hermione* and *Perdita*, her dramatic force was absolutely convincing. The absence of any aggressively amorous episodes in these roles was the reason of her success. Miss Anderson fails utterly when she attempts to interpret any of the characteristics resulting from the dominion of sexuality. You feel that the failure is not due to lack of study, but merely to an inability to express the more subtle shades. Her *Rosalind* is charming; but it is not Shakespeare's *Rosalind*.

It is a *Rosalind* who is by no means passionately in love with *Orlando*.

Miss Anderson is always accompanied on her travels by her fond stepfather, Dr. Hamilton Griffin, a very amusing old gentleman with a colossal business eye. He has steered Miss Mary through many a critical shoal. He has been on hand when, alone, she might have foundered in the dramatic sea. He is very proud of his Mary, and is on more than mere friendly terms with himself. Before Miss Anderson went to England she used to spend a great deal of time in Long Branch, where she owned a charming cottage. But Long Branch has been forgotten. Nice has taken its place. Perhaps Dr. Griffin sighs for the old days. If he does, he bears his affliction very nicely.

Miss Anderson is an indefatigable worker. She never considers herself and her own powers of endurance when she undertakes any enterprize. She will attend rehearsals, when many a "star" would send a substitute in a stage manager; she will drill "supers," and arrange a stage as she thinks it should be arranged.

Miss Anderson has very many admirable traits. Every man or woman who has played in her company has a good word to say for her. She treats her subordinates with charming consideration. She invites confidences, and herself remedies grievances.

One young girl, a member of the company, went to Miss Anderson, on one occasion, and begged for her protection from certain slights to which she had been exposed. The girl was playing a very small part, and was unknown in the theatrical world. Miss Anderson instantly investigated the matter, set everything right, and entreated the girl to let her know if anything of a disagreeable nature should again occur.

Miss Anderson has been married half-a-dozen times—by report. She is one of the women of whom the public is anxious to know more than there really is to know. Miss Anderson is not a bit sensational. She ought to be, but she isn't. Yet Dame Rumor is ever busy. Mary has snubbed the Prince of Wales; she has made all arrangements to enter a convent; she is particularly chummy with this big-wig and that big-wig; she is going to be married to Lord Tomnoddy, or about to retire from the stage and live in seclusion.

Perhaps if Miss Anderson's position were not financially what it is, she might find this craving on the part of the public extremely profitable. But Mary is rich, and if she wishes to retire from the stage she can do so comfortably. Still, she might gratify us occasionally, and give us just a trifle to talk about. Even her recent marriage with Antonio de Navarro, was conducted in a bewilderingly unsensational manner.

AGNES BOOTH.

"I AM a terrible disappointment to interviewers," said Mrs. Agnes Booth one day, as we sat chatting, in her delightful little flat in West Thirtieth street. "In fact, I may say that I am a gigantic failure as far as the interviewing question is concerned."

All of which was, of course, a mistake. Mrs. Booth is a failure at nothing. As an actress she has for years commanded the attention of the metropolis in both her emotional and her comedy work. As a hostess she is the most charming embodiment of tact and grace, putting her visitors at their ease in an incredibly short space of time, and showing an amount of conversational facility that is astonishing, even for an actress. Mrs. Booth is a thoroughly domesticated woman. Few people outside the theatrical profession know very much of her personally. It is their loss, I assure you. Her home is deliciously unostentatious; her methods those of the sedate and accomplished matron. Her husband, John Schoeffel, the partner of Messrs. Abbey and Grau in some of their enterprises, is one of the few theatrical husbands who cannot complain that stage work causes his wife to neglect the duties of the hearth.

"Few people know," said Mrs. Booth during

the course of our talk, "that in my native country, Australia, I was a dancer. It is a fact. I worked fearfully hard at this vocation, practiced six or seven hours a day, and used to dance in Sydney, between the acts. I might have been dancing now," she added with a laugh, "if heart trouble had not rendered it imperative for me to abandon that life. I had heart trouble then, and I have had it ever since. I was passionately fond of dancing. In fact, in Australia, I had not the faintest intention of acting. I had the thorough training of a ballet dancer, and was conversant with all the requirements of that calling. While I was quite young, I went to San Francisco, and danced in opera ballets. I appeared in 'Un Ballo di Maschera' with Adelaide Phillips, I think it was. Yes, my career has been a very checkered one. I like to look back upon its phases."

Mrs. Booth spoke as few actresses speak. She even remembered dates, and spoke unhesitatingly of the sixties. Now it has been my frequent experience that the women of the stage are either unable or unwilling to remember anything further back than ten years. In many cases five years is the extent to which they permit their memories to retrograde.

"I have played nearly every part imaginable," she went on, smiling. "I have played old women when I was a very young one, and before I even played young women. I have almost played old men. My stage experience has been a beautiful mixture."

Mrs. Booth laughed. She really enjoyed her own criticisms of herself. And she was not inclined to be at all flattering. In fact she embarrassed me at times, for I felt that I really ought to deny some of the statements she made about herself.

"For six years I played in San Francisco," she said. "Then I came east and appeared with Mr. Forrest at Niblo's Garden. On the off-nights I played in 'Arrah-na-Pogue.' Then I went to the Boston Theatre and played everything you can possibly think of, and supported nearly everybody you can mention, including Jefferson, Montgomery, and a German actor with an awfully unpronounceable name. I always remember that German gentleman. One night when we were playing, I got a very severe bruise in the face from his spurs. He had to fall on a sofa, and I had to go to him. He fell rather suddenly. His feet went up in the air, and I was hurt. He couldn't speak a word of English. I forgave him. It sounds funny now, but I failed to see the humor of the accident at the time. I came to New York—let me see, how many years ago was it?"

Mrs. Booth covered her face with her hand and reflected. "Sixteen years ago," she said, presently. "I always reckon dates by the age of my son Sidney. He is the landmark for my memory. Yes, I came to New York sixteen years ago, and have remained here ever since, with the exception of three years when I starred. My husband, Mr. Junius Brutus Booth, had lost $100,000 with Booth's Theatre, and I felt that I must do something. It was not at all a pleasant experience. I had four little babies, and I worried and grizzled and pined. I could not stand it any longer, and came home. Then I went to the Union Square Theatre, and appeared in 'The Pink Dominoes,' and later in 'A Celebrated Case' under Mr. A. M. Palmer's management. Then I was seen in 'Sardanapalus' at Booth's Theatre, and in 'Old Love Letters,' 'Champagne and Oysters,' 'Engaged,' and 'Fairfax,' at the Park. After that I went to Mr. Daniel Frohman at the Madison Square Theatre, and appeared there in 'Esmeralda,' also playing in 'Young Mrs. Winthrop.' I left him, and after a few more experiences, joined Mr. A. M. Palmer, opening in 'Sealed Instructions.' I have never left Mr. Palmer. I am with him still."

Mrs. Booth had certainly given a very concise account of herself. Her son Sidney came in at that moment and was affectionately greeted by his mother. He is a comely, frank-looking young man, with a very evident admiration for his accomplished parent.

"People often ask me," said Mrs. Booth, "which I prefer playing—emotional or comedy roles. I tell you frankly that I have no preference in the matter at all. Of course sentiment wears a good deal more than comedy, and I really feel very deeply when I play such emotional parts as those I assumed in 'Jim, the Penman,' and 'Captain Swift.' But I would just as soon play an emotional as a comedy part. It really doesn't matter in the least to me. I have been before the public so long that I have very little pride. Sometimes I think that I am pretty bad in both sentiment and comedy."

This was no little bit of fishing for compliments. From most actresses that is exactly what it would have been. But Mrs. Booth was completely in earnest. All the glamor of the profession seems to have worn off for her. She is artistically matter-of-fact.

"Although I have been before the public so long," she resumed, "I am the most fearfully nervous creature on a first night that you can picture. I am in perfect agony. I never see a soul on first nights except my fellow-actors and actresses. You find it difficult to believe that, don't you? It is a positive fact, I assure you solemnly. A new play is to me a frightful ordeal. I try to reason with myself, but it is not the least use. The present play running at the Madison Square Theatre, caused me a good deal of anguish. I have to sing that song 'If you want to know the time, ask a p'liceman.' I have never sung a note in my life, and am lamentably wanting in that direction. The song was a perfect bugbear to me. It haunted me night and day. I very nearly threw up the part on its account. After one rehearsal I said to my husband, 'John, I think I shall give up my part in "Aunt Jack." That song will kill me!' He wouldn't hear of such a thing, so I determined to make the best of it. I shall never forget the first night of 'Aunt Jack.' It will be the same when we present the play in Boston. I shall not know whether I am standing on my head or my heels. Mr. Palmer often jokes me about this role in ' Aunt Jack,' and another role, that of *Constance* in Shakespeare's ' King John,' of which I was very proud. *Constance* is the best piece of acting I have ever done. It is so utterly opposed to 'Aunt Jack' that to mention these two roles as being played by the same actress is really funny."

Mrs. Booth is very much opposed to the long runs that now prevail at metropolitan theatres. She says that people get so fearfully tired of playing one part night after night for months. This complaint has been made by many people outside of the theatrical profession. But if a manager finds that he can make money with one play for six months, he is not going to the expense and trouble of risking a second. Long runs in a big city, which draw people from the outside as well as from the inside, are inevitable.

I could have stayed and talked to Mrs. Booth for hours. Luckily for her, that was impossible. I am always very careful never to outstay my welcome anywhere, but I really felt a distinct regret at tearing myself away from this brilliant woman's home. I trampled upon my feelings, however, like a veritable martyr, and withdrew in time.

Mrs. Booth is a great favorite with theatrical people. Do you know why? Simply because she never seems to know that she is great. Theatrical people like that kind of a woman, because there are not many such to be found.

I always remember the professional matinée given at the Star Theatre by Mme. Sarah Bernhardt. All the actors and actresses in the metropolis were there. At the conclusion of the performance, a little group of theatrical women stood discussing it. Sarah Bernhardt was not at all kindly criticised. This fault and that fault were discovered in the methods of the *tragedienne*. There was a pretty general sort of a feeling that "we could have done it as well."

But Mrs. Booth was enthusiastic. "I have never before seen anything like it," she said. ".It shows me how little I know, and what a failure I am."

MINNIE PALMER.

SOME years ago I was fortunate enough to attend a meeting held by those vivacious ladies who pretend that they want to vote, and who ask us to believe that they really think themselves to be the equals of men. I was particularly fascinated by the lady who presided, a comely, rosy-cheeked woman, who looked not a day over forty, and who was most artistically attired. Her presidency was most amusing. The poor little woman had heard of the Parliamentary rules of debate, and imagined, I suppose, that she understood them. But her dismay, when half a dozen verbose women spoke at the same time, rose to points of order, objected, and indulged in other of the fascinating luxuries con-

nected with debate, was intense. I felt sorry for her. She didn't look a bit strong-minded. In fact she appeared to be thoroughly ill-at-ease. After I had talked to her for some time, I discovered that she was Mrs. Kate Palmer Stearns, the mother of little Miss Minnie Palmer. Of course I imagined that the president of such a club must naturally despise such frivolities as "soubrettes." I hesitated before even mentioning Miss Minnie. I need not have done so. I soon discovered that Mrs. Stearns was very fond of her daughter. It was "dear Minnie" this, and "dear Minnie" that. She was so lonely when Minnie was away; so happy when she could welcome her home ; so eager to see her on the stage ; so delighted to testify to her improvement ; and so on.

Mrs. Kate Palmer Stearns is quite as interesting as her daughter. I don't feel a bit guilty at having mentioned her here.

Miss Minnie Palmer is a very winsome, amiable little lady, unaffected, blithe and amusing. She has been before the public many years, and folks are inclined to think her older than she really is. Miss Palmer, however, is quite young. I positively decline to mention her age, for her mother's sake. If you had met Mrs. Stearns, you would appreciate my delicacy as it deserves to be appreciated.

Miss Minnie has been more venturesome that other American actresses. She has played in nearly all the English speaking countries on the face of the globe. Her husband, Mr. John R. Rogers, had his own ideas as to the methods of "making" an actress. He set to work, and through his labor Miss Palmer has attained her present position.

John R. Rogers is the most consummate "advertiser" it is possible to imagine. He has a deep and strong-rooted belief in the influence of the newspaper paragraph. He waylays journalists and pours interesting stories into their willing ears; he manufactures pleasant little "yarns;" devises agreeably sensational schemes; there is nothing that he will not do in order to be paragraphed. At one time he has a thrilling story of a detective who passes his life in jealously guarding Miss Minnie's wonderful diamonds; then it is a rumor that Miss Palmer has been robbed by students at the theatre; another time it is the pleasant intelligence that Miss Palmer is spending a month with Queen Victoria's cousin in London.

It is safe to say that no actress was more indulgently treated by the newspapers than Mrs, John R. Rogers. But after a time, this kind of thing became rather sickening. It was fatiguing —this constant Minnie Palmer-ism. Mr. Rogers' methods were soon known, and there was a reaction. The time came when dramatic editors were afraid to use Miss Palmer's name for fear they might be accused of unduly advertising her.

I know of one editor who said to Mr. Rogers, "Johnny, if I heard that the theatre had burned down, with Minnie in it, I should hesitate before using the article, believing it to be one of your clever little advertisements."

Mr. Rogers is personally a very good fellow. He is most devoted to his charming little wife. He is a man of business, against whose reputation for integrity no single word has been spoken. He has made a great deal of money with Miss Palmer. When in the city, Mr. and Mrs. Rogers live in magnificent style. Their home, recently fitted up in the Westminister Hotel annex, is really a sumptuous place.

It is filled with treasures collected from the principal cities of the world, and arranged with perfect taste. Miss Palmer's music-room is a joy. Japanese portières conceal it from the view of the chance visitor. The walls are hung with portraits of the best known composers; the piano is a superb instrument; dainty bric-à-brac, queer little tables, autograph portraits, and ornaments of all descriptions, are to be found everywhere. The carpets, of heaviest velvet, would make a clodhopper's footstep sound fairy-like; tapestry hangings, and beautifully-tinted curtains rendered the apartment most artistic.

The drawing-room is simply gorgeous. It is as full of art treasures as a room destined to be inhabited could be. Rugs, tapestries, lamps, cabinets, silver ornaments, knick-knacks in gold, porcelain, ivory, a Dresden china clock, a bronze statuette of Salome, easels, tables, vases, pictures, portraits of the Prince and Princess of Wales, bisque figures, etchings—all are in this drawing-room. I must say it does credit to the good taste of Mr. and Mrs. Rogers. Many people with plenty of money are not artistic enough to know how to spend it. Nobody can thus accuse either Miss Minnie Palmer or her husband.

In the dressing-room is a cabinet which Mr. Rogers declares was made from wood cut from the ancestral park of Sir Henry A. Clavering. It is certainly a very handsome and unconventional looking piece of furniture.

Mr. Rogers' writing-room is a lovely "den." I should like it for myself. In fact I may say I have been guilty of breaking the tenth commandment and coveting my neighbor's writing-room. That desk ought to be able to inspire priceless thoughts, while the theatrical "trophies" are interesting themes for any number of "special articles." Mr. Rogers has scores of books.

The sleeping-room is as pretty as any other apartment in this charming home. It is furnished in the style favored by Marie Antoinette. Anybody who has visited Versailles will have seen the Marie Antoinette "souvenirs" there. Miss Palmer has copied them as closely as possible.

Miss Minnie reposes beneath blue silk bed coverings, which are adorned with filmy Valenciennes lace. The carpet is deep blue; the hangings are of a corresponding hue.

Mr. Rogers fitted up this home quite recently. He had been storing his treasures; many of them had been for years in safety vaults. Mr. Rogers makes a capital host. He is always very proud of showing his friends through his home.

As an actress, Miss Palmer has improved very much of late. When I first saw her, I wondered at her popularity. She was little more than a boisterous, self-conscious imitation of Miss Lotta. But Miss Palmer is more polished at the present time. Her aims so far have not been of the most elevated order, but I fancy that she is not only capable but anxious to attempt better things than such medleys and concert hall entertainments as " My Sweetheart," and " My Brother's Sister." In fact, Miss Palmer has appeared in legitimate comedy. She made a great success in W. S. Gilbert's " Engaged," and has been seen in other plays. Mr. Rogers told me some time ago that Miss Minnie intended to produce little one-act plays of the style made popular by Miss Rosina Vokes. She will be admirably suited for this kind of work, and I prophesy success if she attempt it. I was very pleased with Miss Palmer in the little sketch entitled " The Ring and the Keeper."

EMMA JUCH.

HERE is a joyous star-spangled-bannerism about Miss Emma Juch that is positively pleasant to contemplate. The days when the divine but dollaresque Patti can float over to American shores and demand five thousand for a single warble, are surely passing away. American singers will soon be recognized all over the world, and even in their own country, I believe. The vocal superiority of the American is being rapidly recognized. And it is just such delightful young women as Miss Emma Juch who will win over the foreignly-disposed minds of their own countrymen.

At the present time Miss Juch is at the head of her own opera company, singing through the United States, and meeting with some success—

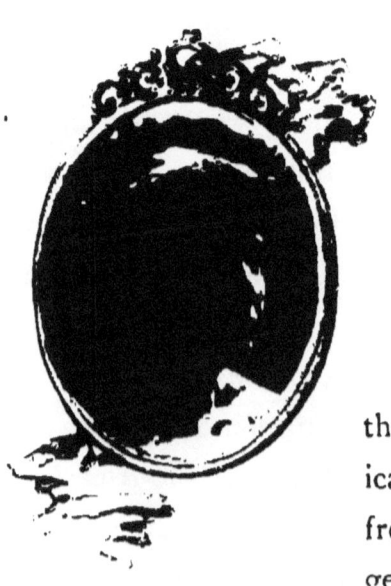

more than might have been expected. I confess that I had very little faith in the success of the organization, even after I had heard it interpret "Mignon," and recognized the excellence of the interpretation. Americans like their song-birds from abroad, glittering with gems presented by European potentates, veneered by the conservatories of London and Paris and Berlin and Vienna, and endorsed by the music-lovers of the old world. And so it is that American girls with splendid vocal equipments cross the ocean and do Europe pretty thoroughly before they venture to set foot again on their native heath. Even then they have to contend with those who have had the advantages of foreign birth.

Now Emma Juch did have that advantage. It was so slight, however, that even her most managerial manager would be unable to avail himself of it. She was born in Vienna while her parents, who were both citizens of the United States, were testifying in a law-suit in that city. Now, it is generally conceded, that though you may be born in a stable, there is no law of logic that will necessarily make you a horse. So Miss Juch, though her birthplace was Vienna, is an American by reason of her American parents. If this is not absolutely clear, I withdraw from the contest, rather than discuss it. An American paper said some time ago: "America may forgive Miss Juch for coming into the world abroad, since she was sufficiently patriotic to be born on the Fourth of July." I hope America will forgive Miss Juch, and will permit her to take that place which would have been hers even before this, had she been what is popularly known as "a foreign artist."

She is an amiable, industrious young woman, and her American traits are at once discoverable in her independence and good-fellowship. Although traveling as an operatic star, she declines to patronize any of the ways of the prima donna. The other day when she was arriving in Washington, her managers sent a carriage to the station to meet her and convey her to her hotel.

"I ride while the members of my company walk?" she asked in surprise. "If the roads are good enough for them, they are good enough for me."

And so the prima donna of the opera company took her way on foot with the most humble members of the organization. This is Americanism of a very pronounced description; so pronounced indeed, that it isn't much practised among the stage people of America.

Miss Juch knew that she had a "voice" at a very early age. Her father, Justin Juch, tried very diligently to nip this knowledge in the bud. He did not like the idea of his daughter becoming a singer, and declined to allow her to study with that end in view. Emma, however, worked quietly at her music, alone. She took lessons, and advanced so rapidly that she was soon asked to take part in a concert given by the pupils of the professor with whom she studied. She made great preparations for this most important event, and fondly imagined that her father knew nothing about them. Mr. Justin Juch was, however, lynx-eyed. He was one of the men in whose household there can be nothing surreptitious.

When Miss Juch appeared at her first concert, she saw, much to her consternation, that her father was seated in the house. He occupied one of the most conspicuous seats, and was glaring. She resolved to win him, and set about the task with a great deal of determination. Papa Juch was very much affected. According to Miss Emma, he arose and left the hall. When his daughter returned home he wept, and kissed her, and declared that he had been very unjust,—and all that sort of thing. Henceforth Miss Juch was not unaided in her struggle for vocal fame. Her father devoted a great deal of his time and money to training her voice. He put her through a severe schooling, and the young girl profited greatly by his teachings. It was Mme. Murio-Celli, however, who trained Miss Juch for her operatic career.

She made her début as a grand opera singer in 1881, as *Filina* in Ambrose Thomas' opera "Mignon," in London, under the management of Col. Mapleson, and during the season sang in "Rigoletto," "The Magic Flute," "Martha," "Faust," "The Huguenots," and "Robert le Diable.' She sang for three seasons under

Mapleson's management. Miss Juch's next engagement was a delightful one for her. She accepted an offer from Theodore Thomas' manager to share the duties imposed upon Mmes. Nilsson and Materna, in the tour of the Wagner artists, Materna, Winkelmann, and Scaria. Miss Juch and Mme. Nilsson sang the role of *Elsa* in " Lohengrin " on alternate nights.

Miss Juch was the first artist engaged for the American Opera Company. She sang in this organization for three seasons, in " The Magic Flute," " Lohengrin," " The Flying Dutchman," " Orpheus," " Nero," and " Faust." In " Lohengrin," when that opera was sung in New York by the American Opera Company, Miss Juch very nearly lost her life by the falling of a heavy piece of iron. The opera had nearly come to an end, and Miss Juch insisted upon finishing it, though she was hurt, and weak from the loss of blood. She remained at the theatre until the final curtain fell.

Miss Juch, during the years she has been before the public, has not been afflicted with too much unoccupied time. Besides appearing operatically, as I have mentioned, she has sung in musical festivals in New York, Boston, Philadelphia, Cincinnati, Chicago, St. Louis and San Francisco, and in such organizations as the New York Philharmonic, the Boston Symphony, the Brooklyn Philharmonic, the Philadelphia Symphony, the Thomas popular concerts, the Gericke orchestral concerts, the New York Liederkranz, and the St. Louis Sængerfest.

Miss Juch has a great future if she is not spoiled or wrongly managed. She is a wholesome, industrious young woman, but she is not a Patti. A great deal of twaddle has been written about Miss Juch. Here is a paragraph that strikes me as being particularly idiotic: "To friends, Miss Juch occasionally tells off charming psychological experiments showing the influence of music upon two pet dogs, Bruno and Dutchie. Possessed of the highest artistic temperament, generous to a fault in giving to the unfortunate and poor, no young woman needing directions as to whither lie the portals of the temple of music, ever yet failed to receive from Emma Juch as much as was in her power to give. To her, beautiful flowers are a mild intoxicant. Hers is literally so Elysian a nature that dumb beasts and children follow with big-eyed faith, and are happiest when near her. But so are all who once have come within the spell of her wonderfully sympathetic voice."

Gracious goodness! and likewise goodness gracious! Miss Juch is a nice, plump, good-looking girl. She needs food a great deal more nourishing than " beautiful flowers," and I am quite sure that she gets it, too. For the benefit of the gentleman who thought that to Emma Juch flowers were a mild intoxicant, I will quote her own words :

"On returning to my hotel after a performance, I partake of a light supper, consisting of cold turkey or chicken, celery, bread, butter and apollinaris water."

A singer who can sit down to cold turkey and celery at midnight, isn't going to be even mildly intoxicated by beautiful flowers. Miss Emma's friends can't succeed in making of her a hothouse plant. She is a comfortable, fragrant, every-day sort of a blossom, excellently trained.

COPYRIGHT BY B. J. FALK.

MARIE JANSEN.

MARIE JANSEN.

AMONG all the comic opera singers of to-day, I do not believe that there is one who has created more of a flutter than the bewitching, little, devilish Jansen, with her naughty, scintillant eyes, her bewildering, laughing dimples, and the poetically rounded limbs that we have all been permitted to discreetly admire. The Jansen is a lady who doesn't appeal to that mighty monster known as general susceptibility. She isn't pretty, she isn't saccharine, she isn't purring, and she isn't wonderfully voiced. Miss Marie is *chic*, piquante, insinuating. There is more of Paris than of New York about her. She is a delight to the educated idea; a suggestion and nothing more, to the gallery god. Marie Jansen, like caviare, is an acquired taste; Lillian Russell, like candy, appeals to the palate of the world. If both these singers were transferred to France, Jansen would be the winner. It would be Marie who would arouse to enthusiasm the *gommeux blasé*; Lillian would have to be satisfied with a less desirable constituency.

Jansen is a sweet, lovable little woman, with sterling qualities; an amusing, wholesome young girl, who can be very much in earnest, and who enjoys life thoroughly, in a perfectly legitimate and enviable manner. Of course, you all know her views on the subject of goodness. They were contained in that inimitable song in "The Oolah." To see the demure, pouting Jansen standing before those admiring maidens, her eyes aglow with deviltry, and that quaint little *je-ne-sais-quoi* pucker at the corner of her mouth, indulging in musical advice, was a privilege that we enjoyed not very long ago.

This is part of her moral :

> Since those days the boys have wooed me; they have bothered and pursued me;
> And I've always tried to do the best I could ;
> And how often, oh, how often, when I've seen their glances soften,
> I have whispered to them warningly, "be good !"
> When your lover urges, presses, tries to dally with your tresses,
> Vows he'd twine them round his heart-strings if he could,
> You will surely be astonished how he's silenced when admonished,
> By the whisper of those mystic words "be good !"

Marie Jansen has not been before the public very long. Nobody can yet say, " Oh, I remember her years ago," as young men about town (bless their dear, fluttering, idiotic hearts !) are so fond of remarking about the divinities of the comic opera stage.

She was born and educated in Boston, and is still very partial to the Hub of the Universe. " My father," she said on one occasion, " wanted me to be a regular Boston girl like other Boston girls, and then settle down and be a regular Boston woman!" Think of a girl with Jansen's eyes and Jansen's disposition settling down into placid, monotonous Bostonianism! She found that she was musical at a very early age, and her father gave her every opportunity to cultivate her talent. He sent her to the New England Conservatory of Music, where she studied long and diligently, finally appearing at concerts in the Hub's Music Hall. Jansen says that it was John Braham who first saw that she was fitted for the stage. She still feels very grateful to John, for it was he who gave her that advice by following which she has become famous.

"He told me that I had a 'stage presence,'" said Jansen. "I didn't know exactly what that was, but I felt it was a nice thing to possess."

Through his influence she was introduced to the manager of the Comley-Barton Opera Company, where she obtained her first position. Her family were very angry at first, as families generally manage to be when circumstances which they have not expected or arranged for, arise. Jansen, however, was all determination. Just study her face a little, if you please, and you will not find this fact a very difficult one to realize. She now declares that she had a sort of a "weeping" for worlds to conquer, and thought that they could best be vanquished from behind the footlights. No regret at her choice has she ever felt. Jansen has conquered a great deal. I will not overwhelm her by declaring that she has nothing more to win. She has, and whatever it be, she will win it.

She first appeared in a musical comedy by Ben Woolf, which was a failure. It was called "Lawn Tennis." Jansen liked it, but the public didn't, which is not the only instance of disagreement between artist and judges. The failure of "Lawn Tennis" however, had no very unfortunate results. The comic opera was withdrawn, and "Olivette" was substituted. Jansen's luck came to her aid. The luck in this case reminds me of the fable of the frog and the naughty boy who pelted it with stones. "What is fun to you," remarked the frog, "is death to me." Miss Catherine Lewis, who was singing the leading role in "Olivette," fell ill, and Marie Jansen took her place, making an immense success.

Later she went with the McCaull Opera Company, where she was very popular.

"I have had the felicity of knowing a score of comic opera queens," said the former manager of that organization to me the other day. "I have suffered, as perhaps few men have suffered, from their whims and caprices. But Jansen—dear little Jansen—she did not cause me a single pang. She never wanted the earth, and she realized that there were other people in the company besides herself."

No higher tribute than this could have been paid to Miss Jansen's nature. Perhaps you don't see the full force of the eulogy, my unsophisticated readers. If you do not, it is because you have never managed a comic opera company. You can congratulate yourselves upon your lucky escape.

Charles Wyndham, the English actor, saw Jansen when she was singing with the McCaull company. He was about to produce at his Criterion Theatre, London, a piece called "Featherbrain," an adaptation of "Tête de Linotte." He remembered Jansen, and sent for her.

"I hesitated very long before I accepted the offer," said Marie. "It was something entirely new to me. I asked the advice of everybody I knew. I was told to go to London. 'You won't have to act,' said one friend, 'you have simply to be Marie Jansen, and that will be all the "Featherbrain" necessary!' I am not sure that this was particularly flattering, but I went to London."

Miss Jansen tells many interesting stories of her London experience. It was the most successful that she has yet had. Mr. A. H. Canby, the manager of Francis Wilson's opera company, told me that Jansen might have made her London visit the event of her life.

"The late John T. Raymond, who saw her in 'Featherbrain,' " he said, " told me that if she had taken his advice, and bought the rights to 'Featherbrain' for America, she would have leaped into the eminence of a successful star on the strength of her artistic performance."

Jansen says that when she reached London she begged Wyndham to announce her on the programmes as " the American actress." Wyndham laughingly advised her not to insist upon this.

" Don't do it," he said. " If you prove to be worthy, people will ferret out all the information they want about you. If you fail to sign yourself 'cyclonically yours,' you'll be glad that you didn't get any sort of prelude."

The patriotic Jansen soon grew homesick.

When Mr. Wyndham put on "The Candidate," and she found that there was no part in it for her, she refused the manager's tempting offer to remain, and returned to America, resuming her position with the McCaull opera company, and finally joining the Casino.

Perhaps it was just as well that Miss Jansen did not buy the "Featherbrain" rights. If she had done so, she would never have appeared in "Nadjy" at the Casino.

Her appearance in "Nadjy" was, like that early experience to which I have already alluded, the result of an accident. Sadie Martinot was to sing the part. She had been extensively advertised. She had taken a trip to Paris, and bought magnificent costumes. But Sadie was too quick-tempered. She quarrelled with the stage manager.

Jansen was just about to indulge in a nice, lazy holiday at her father's country house in Winthrop, when Rudolph Aronson, desperate at the Martinot complication, wrote and begged her to help him. Jansen described her perplexity later to Mrs. Sallie Joy White of the Boston *Herald:*

"I had seen neither the music nor the libretto," she said, "and of course did not know anything about the dance, which was very difficult, and was a special feature of the play. At first it did not seem as though I could do it; it was a tremendous undertaking. But the managers were pledged, they had been to a great deal of expense, and the advertising was tremendous. So to help them out of a bad fix, I undertook the role. How I did work for the next four days! Yes, and nights, too, for that matter, for I took literally hardly no sleep. I worked every minute. I managed the words and the music well enough, but the dancing! I practiced three or four hours at a time, and I gave every minute to it that I could. The exercise was so unusual that it seemed sometimes as though I should drop from sheer exhaustion. I was rubbed after the dancing lesson, to see if I could get a little of the weariness taken out of me, and had it not been for this treatment, I should have been unable to go through such a tremendous physical strain. Of course all my friends were as anxious and as interested as I was, and they all encouraged me with the kindest words and prophecies. The Saturday before the play was to be brought out, I met a friend on the street, who asked me if I was going to be ready. I told him, 'yes.' 'And will the curtain go up sure, on Monday?' he asked, a little sceptically, I thought. I assured him that it would go up at the usual hour, that 'Nadjy' would be played, and that I would play it. 'Plucky girl,' he said, 'we'll all be there to see you.' And so they all were. The house was full. I heartily confess I was very nervous. It was no small matter to take, at four days' notice, the place of one who had made such a study as Miss Martinot had made, and who had been so widely advertised. But I succeeded."

The Jansen attracted a great deal of attention by this performance. Such columns of adulation as those poured upon this effort, it would be hard to duplicate. She laughs at them herself, but she has them all clipped carefully from the newspapers in which they appeared, and pasted neatly in a nice green scrap-book. She showed them to me, and the following rhapsody from the Louisville *Post* is so funny that I can't resist the temptation of giving it verbatim. Here it is: "Marie Jansen—she of the Circe eyes, the ravishing dimples, and poetic legs—was a big favorite with the Louisville folks, but it isn't a marker to what she is with the Gothamites. All of New York almost, from the exclusive 400 to the dregs of the Bowery," (imagine the dregs of the Bowery at the Casino) "nightly worship at her fleshly shrine, and drink in the intoxication of her eye, lip, and limb. In a slightly different way, it is another case of Phryne and the Athenians" (Jansen would have a lovely libel suit) "of Lois and the Carthagenians."

Jansen dotes on all these little tributes to her personality. Here is another item descriptive of Marie at the sea-shore, which certainly deserves to go down to posterity, (of course it will do so in this book). Jansen cut it out with her own fair fingers, and prizes it excessively. It runs as follows :

"That sleepy little settlement bordering on the white sands of Winthrop beach, known as Ocean Spray, has at last a real sensation. It arrived the other day, and has thrown the cottagers into a state of indescribable excitement. The young men of the place are more directly affected by the presence of the invader than are the young ladies, although their sensibilities have received a shock that it will require all the winter months to subdue. Singular as it may seem, the cause of this extraordinary commotion is a little bundle of salmon-colored Japanese silk. What in the world could be found in a package of this kind that its presence has created such a furore? Listen. This flimsy material when examined, shows that it has been made into two garments. There are two pieces: one is a little pair of 'pants,' no more than sixteen inches long, while the other looks like a ballet dancer's dress. Who owns them, and what are they for? Why, that's Marie Jansen's bathing costume—haven't you seen her with it on? No! then go to the beach immediately, and enjoy the sweet divinity when she takes her daily dip in the 'briny.' It is a sight for the gods. Marie has become quite a natatorial expert during her sojourn at Ocean Spray, and enjoys her morning bath as keenly as the small boy who steals from school for a swim. When Nadjy rolls over on her back, and does the floating act, she looks like a small bundle of sunset clouds riding the waters. Her movements are as graceful as a speckled trout's. She's not looking for flies, however. She is satisfied with admiration, and she gets it, too. But the great climax is reached when Marie lifts herself from the waters, and runs up on the beach in search of her long cloak, which she throws over her shoulders after finishing her sport. Of all material, Japanese silk is the most clinging when wet. Is it any wonder then that Marie creates a thrill of admiration among the privileged observers when her pink toes trip along the sea-kissed skirts of the continent?"

Isn't that a gem? I wish to goodness I knew the name of the paper in which it appeared. I wouldn't for the world be accused of trying to purloin such a jewel. Marie laughs at all the witty paragraphs written at her expense. If you could see the gruesome pictures of her that have been published, you would wonder that she could still smile. Many of these pictures look as though they had been sketched in the Chamber of Horrors of the Eden Musée.

But Jansen is a dear, good-natured little girl. She likes newspaper men, as every sensible actress, with an eye to the vast assistance of advertising, should do. When a newspaper man wants opinions on any subject connected with the stage, he flies to Marie Jansen, and the sweet young woman rushes into print, and very cleverly, too.

A Chicago paper asked Jansen for a criticism on Madame Jane Hading. She wrote one, and wound it up as follows:

"An old Irishwoman once said to a party who shall be nameless: 'Ah, sure, thim two eyes wuz niver put in yer head for the good av yer sowl!' Could that woman see Madame Hading, she would, I'm sure, repeat herself. Did you ever see such eyes? I never did, and never shall I forget them. Now, what I've said, may sound like gush, but it isn't; it's honest."

Here are a few lines that Jansen wrote to me:

" I have *never* been married" (a very ferocious

dash under the adverb) "and at present have no desire to be. As to my ambitions—what shall I say? I sometimes think I am one mass of contradiction. When the final verdict is given, however, I should like it to be, 'She has caused more smiles than tears!'"

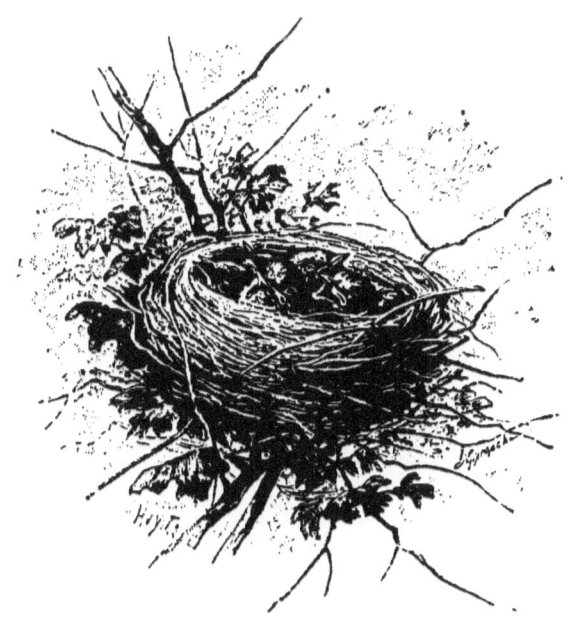

MARIE WAINWRIGHT.

ONE of the actresses who may be described as "getting there," is Miss Marie Wainwright. She was lucky enough to secure a manager who toiled for her with the zeal of an enthusiast, who literally thrust her into the position she now occupies. He is dead now—poor Gus Mortimer. During Miss Wainwright's recent engagement at the Fifth Avenue Theater, he passed away. The play went on just the same. Not a single performance was sacrificed to the memory of its engineer. Truly, there are members of the theatrical profession who lose their charms the instant that the glamor of the footlights is removed.

Miss Wainwright is a very pretty woman, thoroughly educated. She is the daughter of the late Commodore Wainwright and the grand-

daughter of Bishop Wainwright. She was brought up to regard the stage— well, certainly from a discreet distance. Miss Marie was an impulsive maiden, it is said. I find it difficult to believe this, but as I had not the felicity of knowing her in those young days, I must accept what I am told as fact. She married a gentleman named Slaughter, under romantic circumstances, and by him had two pretty daughters. One of them is as tall as Miss Wainwright herself at the present time—a pleasant-faced, amiable-looking damsel. Her father is now dead, and Miss Wainwright is the wife of Louis James, an excellent actor, intelligent and magnetic.

The actress always hád a hankering for the stage. She was a Philadelphia girl, and I can understand Philadelphia people hankering for anything that will take them away from Philadelphia. She used to slip away from home and go to the theatre. Its fascinations tempted her strongly. And when once the fever of the stage seizes you, there is nothing to do but to plunge into its vicissitudes. If you are fortunate, its beauties will still remain; if unfortunate, you will see its emptiness. Under no other circumstances can you obtain this knowledge.

Miss Wainwright was plucky. She has a charming personality. It would have been strange if she had not met with success. There is always hope for pretty women. The public want to see them. It is easier to forgive an awkward manner than an unlovely face. Miss Wainwright made her début at Booth's Theater, appearing with George Rignold as one of his six *Juliets*. Rignold, at his benefit, played *Romeo* with a different *Juliet* every night, and Miss Marie was one of these lucky women.

She was greatly impressed with the part of *Juliet*. Nearly every actress is. It is the most remarkable thing in the world, how women who are unsuited in every way to such parts, long to moan and gurgle and languish as Shakespeare's beautiful Italian. *Juliet* is a disease, a virulent, contagious disease. At times it even becomes an epidemic. Miss Wainwright has recovered from the malady. I believe that sensible Gus Mortimer rooted it out of her. If it could only be eliminated from the systems of a score of actresses at present before the public, how delightful it would be!

After her appearance with Mr. Rignold, Miss Wainwright did some more Juliet-ing at the

Boston Museum. Then she appeared as the *Countess* in " Diplomacy." This she did not like at all. The *Juliet* fever was still raging, and she looked upon it as retrograding to play such a part as the *Countess* in a modern Sardou effort. A great deal of sound advice was lavished upon the ambitious young woman, and such good effect did it have that in a short time she was singing *Josephine* in Gilbert and Sullivan's opera " Pinafore." I believe she was the original *Josephine*. I have never ceased to regret that I did not see the performance. I can imagine that Miss Wainwright must have been delightful in this pretty opera. She considered that she had lost her dignity. She wept bitterly, and made herself thoroughly miserable. It certainly was rather unnatural for a *Juliet* to be capering about as *Josephine*, but it is by just such experiences that an actress is made. Mrs. Agnes Booth would never have been to-day in the exalted position she holds, if her work had not been equally as varied as the instance now under consideration. As I have said elsewhere, Mrs. Booth remarked to me, "I have played everything—almost old men."

Miss Wainwright was a very successful *Josephine*. She played the part for nineteen weeks. It was her first and last experience in comic opera. After that she went back to the "legitimate" and stayed there. She first met Mr. James, now her husband, while playing in "The Exiles." She then went with him to Lawrence Barrett's company, where the two remained for a long time.

But Miss Wainwright was very ambitious, and it was not long before she was attacked by the starring mania. This purely theatrical malady must have treated her very cruelly. She was unable to resist its influence, and it was not long before she had the felicity of seeing her own and her husband's name in flaming letters on the posters of the city's highways. Mr. and Mrs. James met with much success. Their work was very excellent. I saw her as *Lady Teazle*, and enjoyed the performance very much indeed. One day Broadway gloated over the rumor that Mr. and Mrs. James were to separate theatrically; that is to say, he was to head one company, and she another. I spoke to Gus Mortimer, their manager, about it.

Said he, "You see she doesn't care to play second fiddle to him in certain plays, and he doesn't care to appear in a similar position with regard to her in other plays. Hence the separation."

Can you, my untheatrical readers, understand such a condition of things? If you are able to do so, you will astonish me greatly, for it is only after long and varied experience with the eccentric beings of the stage, that I have been able to master their whims and their caprices. I nevertheless found it almost impossible to understand this case. Here was a married couple, appearing before the public in the leading roles of their plays, positively jealous of each other. She didn't like to see him take precedence in certain parts; he hated to subordinate himself to her. The partnership made money. It was a sheer case of that fearful vanity that rages behind the footlights. It makes brutes of men whom the public only see smiling and smirking in their *rouge* and their finery; it converts into veritable demons the apparently guileless, lovable women who impersonate the models of feminine virtue and heroism that the playwright paints.

The separation took place, and the husband and wife are now in different companies. She has nobody who can possibly draw a grain of attention from herself; he is the lord and master of his organization. I hope they like it. I can't help thinking that the public have a sneaking regard for a husband and wife in a single company. Every kiss he gives her they look upon (foolishly, of course) as an evidence of sincere, legitimate love; every fond glance she casts in his direction they like to believe (wrongly, of course) is genuine and proper.

Miss Wainwright's *Viola* in " Twelfth Night " is a beautiful piece of work. Her recent engagement at the Fifth Avenue Theatre was probably a financial success. As I said, the actress is " getting there." She suffers a great deal from self-consciousness, but I presume that this defect will be remedied as time rolls on. She is shapely and pretty, and is aware of both facts. When she appeared as *Rosalind* in " As You Like It," her manager was particularly careful to circulate some dainty little stories about the Ganymede dress she would wear. It was a delicate way of calling attention to Miss Wainwright's shapeliness. These dainty little stories, however, were not received with the undisguised pleasure expected. There are several actions favored by Miss Marie in the male episodes of *Rosalind* and *Viola*, that might more gracefully be omitted

There are, however, many theatre-goers who only endure these roles for the sake of the revelations that they make possible. The "doublet and hose" ought to be absolutely delicate. Any interpretation which robs *Viola* and *Rosalind* of any of this delicacy is un-Shakesperian.

Miss Wainwright has a brilliant future. Her defects are few, and they can all be remedied.

LOUISE BEAUDET.

A DEFTLY arranged crown of copper-tinted hair; a row of pearl-white teeth perpetually revealed by an irresistible smile; a trim little figure, which the people who try to eschew English would call *petite;* and a creamy complexion unmarred by "make-up" of any sort, formed a combination of pretty characteristics that I saw one morning at the Hotel Belvedere, when I called upon Miss Louise Beaudet. In fact they existed in Miss Louise Beaudet, the vivacious little comic opera singer, whose art was revealed most conspicuously to New Yorkers when she sang the role of *Chilina* in "Paola" at the Fifth Avenue Theatre, with the Duff comic opera company, not very many months ago.

Miss Beaudet has already had a very checkered  career, though she is still young and—I was going to say foolish. Well, I will say it, because I consider that winsome little Louise has not thoroughly realized her own artistic worth as a comic opera singer, or she would never have spent years playing Shakespearian roles, and courting comparison with artists who had made them a specialty. Of course she told me that she didn't know what to say about herself, and equally of course, I found, with a little cross-examination, that she did.

I drew her out gradually, and she proved to be quite interesting. "Of course you know that I am French," she began. I didn't, and I could hardly believe it, as her English is perfect, with no foreign accent whatever. "I was born in Tours, France, and I came to America with my parents when I was a little bit of a child. When the 'Pinafore' craze was at its height, I appeared in one of the juvenile companies, at fourteen years of age. After that Mr. Duff began a search for a girl that could sing the role of the *Duchess* in 'The Little Duke,' and look very young at the same time—a combination that was not the easiest thing in the world to discover. I had been singing for a few months, and it seemed that I was just what he wanted. So he engaged me, and thus it was that my stage career really began."

Miss Beaudet folded her hands, sat bolt upright, and adopted a pertly fascinating look that I should very much like to have captured for a picture.

"I was in luck," continued Miss Beaudet.

"'The Little Duke' was produced at Booth's Theatre, and Mme. Aimée, who was going to present the opera in French, saw it. She and her manager, Mr. Grau, liked my performance, and engaged me for the French production. So I created the part of the *Duchess* in New York in English and in French, and at the same theatre. It was really strange. I had even the same dressing-room for both productions. I enjoyed the French production immensely. I was speaking my mother-tongue, and it seemed delightful to me. I was completely infatuated with the stage, and my early education had not taught me that there was anything objectionable about it, as most American girls learn to believe. To be an artist is, in France, a very great thing, and of course I wanted to be an artist. We all do."

Miss Beaudet laughed in a very kittenish way —that is to say, if a kitten ever laughed, which is open to question, it would laugh just as did Miss Beaudet.

"The first time I ever went to the theatre," she said, "my mother took me to the Comédie Française, and I longed to play one of those lovely parts. But to continue: I stayed six months with Mme. Aimée. She was very, very charming. I owe everything to Aimée—poor Aimée! She did not seem to look upon me as a member of her company. I was very young, and she was very attached to me. She taught me her parts. When she was in San Francisco she was prostrated by a very severe cold. She knew it was coming on, and she instructed me in her part without saying a word to anybody. I had a rehearsal with the leader of the orchestra, and Mme. Aimée then told Mr. Grau that she would be my sponsor. I was only a child. Grau couldn't believe that Aimée was in earnest. But she was, and I had the honor of appearing as *Serpolette* in 'Les Cloches de Corneville.' She taught me four of her parts. I can never forget her. Anything that I have ever done in comic opera I owe to Aimée."

Miss Beaudet lost herself in meditation for a few moments. Apparently they were not of the most cheerful nature. She appeared to be thinking about less pleasing incidents in her stage career.

"I left the comic opera stage," she said suddenly, "and went into the drama. My voice seemed to have given out. I suppose that I sang too much at a time when any undue strain upon the voice would be likely to prove dangerous. In San Francisco I joined the Baldwin stock company. I was the *ingénue*. I studied Shakespeare diligently, and by those wonderful plays I perfected myself in the English language. It was the best schooling I ever had. It was a great company. Clara Morris and other stars would come to San Francisco, and we would support them. But I had become a roamer, and I did not stay in California. I went to Australia, India, China and Japan, playing Shakespearian parts. I have been more varied than you could possibly imagine. I dearly loved *Juliet* and *Rosalind* and *Portia* and *Desdemona*. Physically I think this arduous work injured me, but it was an education, and an education that will benefit me even now, when I have returned to the comic opera stage, and am not likely to try Shakespeare again. I like to remember my success in the far-off lands, and I can do so by these souvenirs."

Miss Beaudet showed me an enormous portfolio containing newspaper clippings culled from India and China.

" On one occasion, in Calcutta," she said, " I played *Hamlet*—yes the role of the melancholy Dane—and at the close of the entertainment I sang portions of Patience.' Read this : ' We had hardly recovered from our amazement, when she sang *Patience*. She had divested herself of the depths of manly passion, and stood before us as a pretty dairy-maid.' In Shanghai I made a speech, which was a great hit. The newspapers treated me most kindly. While abroad I made a few attempts at comic opera, and sang in 'La Grande Duchesse'—I blush to think of it; and my pet part, that of *Rose Michon* in 'La Jolie Parfumeuse.' Was I not versatile?"

I was bound to admit that she was. So much variation in such a little lady seemed almost impossible.

"I do not think that I am destined for a *Juliet*," she went on. "Americans want large, lovely women, and they have Mary Anderson. I am afraid that I should never be remembered in this country for my Shakespearian work, but before returning to comic opera, I indulged once more. Mr. McVicker, of McVicker's Theatre, Chicago, was going to produce 'The Tempest,' and I made up my mind to study the part of *Ariel*. I played the part, and I enjoyed it thoroughly. It was very, very difficult, but oh! so lovely."

Miss Beaudet clasped her hands, and then, with pardonable femininity, produced a photograph of herself as *Ariel*, and asked me to look at it.

"I think that *Ariel* is one of the most beautiful parts that Shakespeare ever wrote," she said. "It is certainly the most poetical to my mind. I believe that I appreciated it more than anything I had ever played. Chicago was very kind to me, and one writer in particular was certainly flattering."

She gave me a slip from a newspaper, and turned away with an assumption of coyness, while I read a description of herself. It was beautiful, yet Chicago-esque. In fact I cannot refrain from reproducing it. "Her complexion is clear, but pale, and her large eyes are dark brown—the wave-washed onyx that goes with genius! Her rich brown hair, seeming as if sprinkled with gold dust, is brushed well back over the pale, intellectual forehead, and provides an excellent setting for regular features and a face of rare animation!"

The *Journal* gentleman certainly surpassed himself in his adjectival eloquence. I told Miss

Beaudet that it was indeed truly beautiful, and she laughed, though she dearly appreciated the compliments.

"Then," she resumed, "I returned to comic opera. My voice had come back to me, and my friends told me that comic opera was my forte, if I had any. Friends are so funny. Sometimes they tell you one thing; sometimes another. However, I intend remaining in comic opera now, and am really going to settle down, and find a resting place for the sole of my foot. I still consider France my home, but I am an American citizen, with full rights to enjoyment of the privileges of Uncle Sam's country. I took out naturalization papers two years ago. Yes, I am very proud of being an American, I can assure you, though I still love dear old France. I suppose I can love France, and still be loyal to my adopted country, can't I ?"

Miss Beaudet arched her eyebrows in naïve inquiry. I hastened to assure her that nobody who had spent five minutes in her society would venture to accuse her of treason.

"I frequently take a run over to my native country. My mother, who lived here for a number of years, returned to France, and her dutiful daughter visits her whenever she can spare the time. I have travelled so much that a trans-Atlantic crossing is not a very formidable undertaking for me. I should love to play in France. That is really one of my ambitions. Before I became an American citizen, I had an offer to return to France, with prospects that might have resulted in a pleasant engagement there. I did not know what to do, or how to decide. I didn't want to give up America, and I hated to let the French opportunity slip through my fingers. So I did what women are very fond of doing— asked everybody's advice, determined to adopt that which I considered most agreeable. My friends told me to stay in America by all means. They said that I had already done a great deal of work here, and had been very kindly received. They thought it would be folly on my part to begin all over again in France, where I had never appeared. So I followed this advice. I still hope that one day I may get an opportunity to appear in my native country. But in the meantime I am making the most of my opportunities in this country, and am not going to let them be disturbed by any idle dreams that may, after all, never be realized."

"And do you like the life of a comic opera singer?" I asked. My interrogations had been very few, and I felt that I could not tear myself away without a questioning word.

"Do I like it? It is delightful to me. There is variation, and there is not very much hard work. It is a pleasure to me to sing. Then New Yorkers treated me very kindly. I have just been singing *Pitti-Sing* in 'The Mikado.' I almost cried when Mr. Duff gave me the part. But it was well received, and I am not sorry that

I sang it. I ought to be satisfied. I have good friends and good opportunities. What more does a girl need?"

I didn't know.

PHOTO BY FALK.

PAULINE HALL.

PAULINE HALL.

SOMETIMES I am inclined to believe that if the dignified but symmetrical Goddess of Liberty chose to desert the pedestal from which she surveys the incoming and outgoing vessels in New York Bay, to mundanely seek a position in a comic opera company, her success in that walk of life would be nothing but a question of time. You see, she has plenty of shape, which seems to be the main qualification for the career of a comic opera "star," nowadays.

I am not at all sure that if the queenly (I say "queenly" because in this case I wish to be conventional,) Pauline Hall had been less superbly fashioned from a physical point of view, she would be in the elevated position she now graces. The dudelets and the golden youths of the great American metropolis would not be paying out papa's money for the privilege of watching the beautiful Pauline at the Casino ; nor would the dear old glistening bald-heads be fighting for the front seats, and, in ecstatic scrutiny, flinging bouquets at the feet of Miss Hall.

The comic opera world is an eminently peculiar one. It is governed by other rules and regulations than those which prevail in the legitimate dramatic fields. Vocal merit is not necessarily an essential in the success of a favorite. Of course it hastens the desired result. But given a handsome woman, with a knack of keeping herself before the public, and it is tolerably easy to speculate upon her chances.

When Apothecary Schmidgall of Cincinnati saw his little dark-eyed daughter artlessly frolicking in her western home, I am quite sure that never in his most prophetic moments, could he have pictured her established in a metropolitan suite of rooms, calmly deigning to recognize her own success. I used the word "frolicking." It sounds rather grotesque applied to the statuesque Miss Pauline Hall. As easy would it be to imagine my friend the Goddess of Liberty pirouetting upon her pedestal.

Miss Hall was *née* (as they say in the society papers) Pauline Frederica Schmidgall. It is a melancholy fact that we are none of us able to regulate our own surnames. We are born, surnamed ; all we can do is to rectify the error when we reach years of discretion. John Brodrib was of the opinion that his name displayed on London play bills would hardly be inviting, so he became Henry Irving. Pauline Frederica Schmidgall was evidently of a similar mind. The Schmidgall has faded into deserved oblivion. Pauline Hall is now before us. Long may she remain!

Cincinnati, as I have already hinted, had the honor of supplying us with Pauline. New York is proverbially selfish. In the teeming contest for a World's Fair that was recently so vigorously waged, New York attempted to down every other city. Now, I hold that in return for the inestimable boon of Pauline Hall, New York ought to have gracefully resigned all her claims to the World's Fair in favor of Cincinnati.

I believe in reciprocity. I am quite sure that not one of my readers will venture to assert that Pauline Hall isn't worth at least half a dozen World's Fairs.

Miss Hall is about thirty years of age, plump, pretty, and well-formed. Her large, lustrous eyes are perhaps her greatest charm, though her shapeliness is admired by all. Miss Hall looks even more charming in the street than she does on the stage. She is one of the few women who have the knack of knowing what clothes suit her best, and of wearing those clothes. She is a model of sedate luxury; a walking essay on the absurdity of over-dressing. If you met her on Broadway you would notice her garments because they are so beautifully made, and because you have an artistic eye. The masses would pass her by, because she doesn't wear greens, and blues, and flaming reds, and diamonds. But if she doesn't wear diamonds, she has them. Ah! my dear young friends, I wish you had as many. I, myself, would be satisfied with just half.

Pauline became stage-struck in the year 1875. Please recollect that year. Write it in letters of red upon the tablets of your mind. She was first seen in a ballet, in a play produced under the management of Colonel R. E. J. Miles, of Cincinnati. Yes, fifteen years ago Pauline Hall was one of a number of young Terpsichorean bread-earners, dancing in Cincinnati. Colonel Miles evidently recognized the possibilities of a career or the stately Pauline. Her next engagement was also under his management. She traveled with the American Racing Association and Hippodrome, posing in tableaux and being otherwise ornamental. Then she joined the Alice Oates opera company, and appeared in a piece called " Folly."

Many of my readers may be surprised to know that Miss Hall has appeared in legitimate drama. She "supported" Mary Anderson (lucky Mary to have such a beautiful pillar to lean upon!) I never saw her when she played with Miss Anderson. In fact I can hardly realize that she could have been *Lady Capulet* in " Romeo and Juliet," and the *Widow Melnotte* in "The Lady of Lyons." But she impersonated both of these creations.

Miss Hall was a member of Rice's Surprise Party in "Pop;" she was seen in " Orpheus and Eurydice " at the Bijou in 1883 ; in " Bluebeard," in "The Seven Ravens," and in 1885 in " Ixion." Miss Hall has even sung in German. She was heard in the "Fledermans" at the Thalia Theatre in 1885. But her first actual success was made at the Casino, and she has remained at that theatre since 1886. Miss Hall's voice is not at all extraordinary. In fact it is somewhat metallic in quality. Her dramatic powers are by no means great. She walks gracefully through her parts, filling the eye with her personal charms. As I hinted before, however, the public often receives a handsome woman better than it does a talented one..

Says Reid: "All the objects we call beautiful agree in two things, which seem to concur in our sense of beauty. First, when they are perceived, or even imagined, they produce a certain agreeable emotion or feeling in the mind; and, secondly, this agreeable custom is accompanied with an opinion or belief of their having some perfection or excellence belonging to them."

So when we see Pauline Hall in her sumptuous Casino garbs, when we notice the lustrous dark eyes, and the tumultuous beauty of her form, we are tempted to believe that her voice is purer than it really is, and that her dramatic powers are greater than in our cooler moments, removed from her personality, we would care to admit them to be. We are all so disgracefully human where a pretty woman is concerned.

Pauline Hall is rich, but unlike those stage favorites who live stupidly in the present, and fritter away the wealth that pours in upon them, Miss Hall casts one of those lovely eyes of hers in the direction of the future. She is a sensible woman, and a shrewd one. She is said to be worth about $100,000, which she has most profitably invested. One of these days she will retire. The career of a comic opera singer is a short one. The more famous she happens to be, the shorter her career. A quick fire burns itself out more rapidly than a slow one. Miss Hall realizes this. Should she retire at the present time, she could live comfortably for the rest of her days. But she will probably remain with us for some years to come. Her voice, at the present time, is better than it has ever been.

Miss Hall lives very quietly when she is in the city. She has a little flat in West Thirty-Fifth Street near Seventh Avenue, and lives there with " Dora," a secretary and "general manager." Miss Hall was at one time married to Mr. Edmund R. White, who was known as "a man about town," and whom she first met in San Francisco in 1878, and later in St. Louis.

But Miss Hall tired of being Mrs. White. She secured a divorce, one of the grounds for which was (no, don't laugh) non-support. Yes, Mrs. Pauline Hall White declared that her husband didn't support her. She obtained her freedom and I don't think she will be foolish enough to forfeit it again. I hope not, for the sake of the man. The husband of a comic opera "queen" has my most sincere sympathy. If Mr. Fox were alive, I would suggest that he include all

such husbands in a revised edition of his
"Book of Martyrs."

Miss Hall thoroughly recognizes the necessity
of always keeping her name before the public.
She likes people to know where she spends her
summers, and how she is cultivating her voice,
and other equally interesting facts concerning
herself.

To meet, she is most charming. She can
always furnish a topic of conversation, and will
invariably say something amusing.

She is kind hearted and womanly. Her
brother, Fred Hall, was a member of the Casino
company, probably at her instigation. The
young fellow died a few weeks ago, succumbing
to the disastrous weather of 1889 and '90. Miss
Hall was at his bedside night and day, giving up
her own engagements, and devoting herself
exclusively to her brother. She nursed him
carefully, and was with him when he died. A
better sister surely never lived. I like to think

of this trait in Miss Hall's character, and to show you that a popular comic opera prima donna need not necessarily forget the instincts of gentler womanhood.

As a rule it is only the frivolities of a metropolitan favorite that reach the public ear.

MARION MANOLA.

I HAD a nice long talk with little Miss Marion Manola the other day. I called upon her at the handsome house No. 42 West Thirty-Fourth street and had quite a pleasant chat. The Manola is a quiet, unaffected young woman, with no "frills" about her constitution. In the street, she isn't a bit "actressy;" she doesn't paint, she doesn't overdress, she doesn't flaunt. When she is not upon the stage she is Mrs. Mould, invariably accompanied by her pretty little nine-year-old daughter, whose age she candidly tells, without a blush and without the least hesitation.

It was this damselette who asked me to

excuse "mamma" for a few minutes, and who spoke to me as though we were the oldest and best of friends.

I excused "mamma" very readily, and she did not keep me waiting very long. She entered the room, greeted me cordially, and before I could realize the fact, we were in the midst of an entertaining talk.

"I always feel," said Miss Marion, "that I am going through life on a rush. I have no time for anything. Singing every night and rehearsing every day—that is my yearly routine. Yes, I like it, of course. I agrees with me."

It certainly did. Miss Manola was the picture of health. She had none of the lanquid can't-help-it-ism that the prima-donna loves to affect.

She was happy. She was talking to somebody who was going to write something about her, and she let me see that it pleased her. Sensible woman! I admire that kind of candor. I despise the woman who says to you, "Don't write a word of what I have said," and who cuts you dead the next time you meet her, because you followed these instructions.

"I have been very lazy to-day," said the Manola, "I have only just come down-stairs" (it was two o'clock in the afternoon), "and I have been taking my breakfast and luncheon as one meal. Isn't that really very dreadful when you remember that I have a daughter growing up, ready to follow bad examples?"

She laughed, and I, not having an answer ready, did likewise. It is always safe to laugh at anybody else's humor. People appreciate such laughter a great deal more than a witty response, or a sparkling bit of repartee. I asked the Manola to tell me something about her stage career. She seemed rather frightened. I put her at her ease by informing her that I knew all about it, but yearned for her own personal narration.

"I haven't any stage career," she declared rather ruefully. "I have really only been before the public for five years. You don't mean to say you'd like to know where I was born?"

I asserted that I pined for this little scrap of knowledge.

"Well I don't know that I need mind confessing," she remarked after a pause. "My name was Stevens. I was born in Oswego. No, please don't laugh, Oswego is a lovely place—grand, beautiful and all that sort of thing. At any rate, if it were the most odious town on the surface of the globe, I can't help it. I was born there."

Miss Manola seemed to be positively defiant. She looked at me as if she were saying "The murder is out. Now condemn me." I comforted her quietly, and suggested that everybody couldn't be born in London and Paris and New York. Oswego was rather a pleasing birthplace.

" I used to act a good deal in private theatricals in Cleveland," she said, "and when society turned out to be amused, I generally managed to be one of the amusers. I sang in ' Pinafore, as an amateur, and worked really very hard. But there was not much satisfaction in it. I was very ambitious. I longed to go upon the stage, as nothing less than a grand opera singer. Comic opera? No indeed. It never entered my mind. I yearned for grand opera. The dream of my life was to appear as Marguerite in ' Faust,' with two lovely golden pigtails, and a sweet white frock."

Miss Manola's first hopes seemed to rise before her eyes—spectre-like, as the penny-dreadfuls say. She sighed a little, and frowned a little, and bit her lip a little, and reddened a little.

"I went to Paris," she resumed, "and took lessons with the famous Madame Marchesi. I told her, of course, that I wanted to be a grand opera singer, and desired that she should train my voice with that end in view. How I worked. I had to be at her house at nine o'clock every morning, and I stayed there until one in the afternoon. Then I went home and practised there for two hours. I really devoted all my time to the study of music. Some people can harrow up their souls by remembering lost opportunities. I am thankful to say that I cannot do this. I made the most of my time. Madame gave me lessons for nine months. Her teaching was excellent, but she had one fault. She pays too much attention to the high notes of the voice, and too little to the middle register. Marchesi dotes on high notes. I heard one of her pupils the other day. She sang her high notes charmingly, but the middle register was really melancholy. I believe I should have known Marchesi's pupils, even if I had not been informed of that fact before I heard her."

Miss Manola's criticism was good, as far as the young woman she mentioned was concerned.

"When I left Marchesi," she said, "I went to England. My husband, Mr. Mould, known upon the stage as Carl Irving, had lost his money—what little he had—and I was obliged to do something there and then. All my hopes of grand opera had to be put aside. I was only too glad to take the first engagement I could get. It nearly broke my heart. I had such a very excellent opinion of my own ability, don't you know?"

She smiled, a little bitterly, and I allowed her to proceed without interrupting her story.

"I accepted a position with Lingard and Van Biene's comic opera company, and was cast for an important part in 'Falka.' I really was very lucky, though I did not think so at the time. Most girls have to serve an apprenticeship in the chorus, or in very small parts, before they have any opportunity to really sing. I served no such apprenticeship. I was never in the chorus in my life. I made my first appearance with my husband in 'Falka,' at Bath, and met with the approval of the management, though I was by no means an extraordinary success. Lingard and Van Biene wanted to make me sign a contract for five years. I needed the money that such an engagement would bring me, badly enough, but I could not sign such a contract. I was very unhappy. My comic opera surroundings were very new to me and not particularly pleasant. Then I was miserable in England. As I told you, I had never been on the stage in my own country. I longed to get back to America. My husband was quite as anxious as I was to leave England. So we said good-bye to Albion, sailed for Uncle Sam's shores, with some very nice letters from our managers, and were fortunate enough to secure an engagement at the Casino."

Miss Manola, however, did not seem to have looked upon this as a piece of good fortune very long.

"I was not a success at the Casino," she declared, very emphatically. "I went to Chicago with the company, and the newspapers pitched into me so fiercely that I really wished I had never been born."

The idea of Miss Marion reading adverse criticisms, her short hair standing on end, and the longing for death paling her face, was slightly amusing, and I could not repress a smile. She smiled, too. It was an experience not at all unpleasant to look back upon from the security of present success.

"I had no confidence in myself," she said. "That may sound strange to you, but it is a fact. I liked my own voice, but not as much as I did before I had made my first appearance. I have found that confidence is absolutely necessary to success, on the comic opera stage, at any rate.

If you feel that you are going to sing a part creditably, you will sing it creditably. If you predict failure, failure it will be. That has been my experience. I always say to myself now before I sing a new part, 'Manola, that suits you admirably. You are going to make a great hit.' Confidence is everything. Well, I felt I was such a failure at the Casino that I sent in my resignation to Mr. Aronson. I really hoped and half believed that it would not be accepted. But it was. Oh! the blow to my pride! when I knew that they were willing to lose me! I could have fainted, so great was my anguish. The exalted opinion of my own ability that I had once held, was lost forever."

Such blows to vanity are often the salt of life, spurring men and women on to greater efforts. But I did not say this to Miss Manola. I felt that she would not agree with me. After all, it is the kind of salt that we none of us want.

"Then I joined the McCaull Opera Company,

with which organization I remained for four years—up to the present time in fact. I was very happy with this company. I had lovely parts to sing, and I believe I appeared in sixteen or seventeen operas. 'Boccaccio' was the opera in which I felt I did best. The people were all very kind to me. I was completely at home."

"And your grand opera hopes?" I suggested.

"They are still with me," she said, laughing. "I still trust that the day will come when I can be *Marguerite*. I have not forgotten the golden pigtails and the white dress. I believe that my voice would suit the role very well. Grand opera, however, appears to have gone out of fashion, doesn't it? It is a dreadful thing that such should be the case, is it not? But I think that it will be as popular as it once was before long. I do not regret my comic opera life. Not a bit of it. The financial inducements have been very great. Comic opera singers are very well paid, and as they nearly all of them want money, they are generally satisfied with their lot. The excellent remuneration of the comic opera stage is a great thing in its favor, as far as we are concerned. One gets careless, however, perpetually singing in comic opera. It does not give much scope to the voice. I like florid, difficult music, but this belongs very seldom to comic opera, so I have to reserve my florid, difficult efforts for my own personal edification."

"You sing for your own amusement?"

"I am always singing," she replied. "I sing things that I think will improve my voice. I really love music."

There was a piano in the room, and I half hoped that Miss Marion would trill something for my delectation. But I did not venture to suggest this to her, so she will probably be surprised when she learns that I craved a few notes. I felt, however, that if I stayed much longer that I should be unable to refrain from making the request. So I delicately led the conversation to the weather, and from the weather to the door there is but a short step.

EFFIE ELLSLER.

LITTLE Miss Effie Ellsler is, in private life, Mrs. Frank Weston. She is married to an actor, who, in comparison with herself, is big and burly; and it is his name that she assumes at all times except in the theatre. Miss Ellsler is an unpretentious little lady, who goes quietly through the world, playing through the United States during the theatrical season, and spending the rest of the year with her mother. Such a theatrical family as it is, too! First of all, there is Miss Effie's father, John Ellsler, who is still an actor of repute, generally a member of his daughter's company, but who has appeared with all the great stars, and who travelled with Joseph Jefferson through the South as his partner. Then there is Miss Effie's mother, once an actress, known in her girlhood as Miss Murray, later as Mrs. Myers, and finally as Mrs. Ellsler. Mr. and Mrs. Ellsler met at Foster's Theatre in Philadelphia, and were married. Then there is Miss Annie Ellsler, who has also been on the stage, and who sings charmingly; and goodness knows how many boy Ellslers. I have tried to count them, but I get fearfully "mixed" in the attempt. Whenever I see the Ellslers I always think of the song that used to be popular in London, and that rejoiced in this refrain:

> "We are a merry family,
> We are—we are—we are."

I called upon Miss Effie Ellsler a short time ago at the Ashland House, where the family generally stays. While I was waiting for Miss Effie, I heard the following little bit of conversation between Frank Weston and Miss Fannie Hurlick, one of Miss Ellsler's friends:

"Oh," exclaimed Miss Hurlick, enthusiastically, "your wife is a charming little thing, Mr. Weston. Such a sweet little lady! I assure you that I am quite in love with her."

"So am I," replied Mr. Weston, bowing.

That was of course very pretty. The husbands of actresses as a rule generally parade their affection for—well, perhaps I had better not say it. It would be uncharitable.

Little Miss Ellsler came in a moment later from rehearsal, looking as dainty as a spring flower, and as unruffled as a summer lake. She wore a dark green cloth dress, tailor-made (oh! of course tailor-made!) and a little impudent hat of the kind that the English call "pork-pie." There was nothing conspicuous or in the least actress-y in her attire. Her manner was easy and unconventional. I remarked as much to her, and she laughed.

"I have no eccentricities at all," she said. "I am just plain, every-day Effie Ellsler. You never see my name in the papers, except in connection with my stage work, do you? No, I am quite sure you don't. I never do things,—you know what I mean! I don't know why it is, but I like to pass my life quietly, and when not on the stage devote myself to my family. The newspapers treat me beautifully, and I always flatter myself that I appeal to them on my merits. You would be astonished if I told you how few newspaper men I know. It is not because I do not wish to know them, but because—well, you understand—because, as I said before, I am plain, every-day Effie Ellsler."

Mrs. Weston smiled at her husband, but he was busy in conversation with a young actor who had just entered the parlor.

"My husband and I," she said, "have not been

separated for any length of time since we have been married. We met in the theatrical profession, and we always appear together: I believe with Mrs. Kendal, that actors should marry actresses, and actresses should marry actors. I also think that if an actress marry a man who is not in the profession, she ought to leave the stage at once. It is her duty to her husband, and the only way in which she will be able to find married happiness. But, you know, I like to see a married couple on the stage. There used to be an absurd idea that an actress became uninteresting to the public as soon as she was married; that people did not care to see her when she had a husband. That time has passed. Nay, I believe that people are positively attracted toward a married couple on the stage. It is nice to know that the clever actor and the talented actress who seem to be in such excellent accord are in reality husband and wife. Look at Mr. and Mrs. Kendal, Mr. and Mrs. W. J. Florence, Mr. and Mrs.

Barney Williams, and Miss Claxton and her husband. There are instances for you."

Little Miss Ellsler became quite interested on the subject, and it was only by an effort that I could wean her from it, and lead to her stage career, of which I wanted to hear.

"Mine is such a thoroughly theatrical family," she said, "that I can hardly speak of going upon the stage. I was really born into the theatrical profession. I think that I made my first appearance as the child in 'A Sea of Ice.' Then I played the child part in 'Ten Nights in a Barroom,' and *Eva* in 'Uncle Tom's Cabin.' Yes, I was one of the army of *Evas* with which the United States has been invaded. I had to do my little turn, of course. After I had played these baby roles, I went to school. My stage education began in the stock company of my father's theatre in Cleveland. I was pushed more rapidly than you can imagine. Very few people nowadays know that I was educated for the operatic stage."

I didn't know it myself. Miss Ellsler surprised me. She laughed at my look of amazement.

"Don't be so terribly astonished," she said. "My career has been a very varied one. Yes, I made my first appearance on the operatic stage as *Arline* in 'The Bohemian Girl.' Then I sang in 'Martha' and 'The Daughter of the Regiment.' I used to devote my time to singing in these operas, and playing such parts as *Rosalind* in 'As You Like It,' and *Portia* in 'The Merchant of Venice.' A varied career? Yes, indeed. I have sung *Josephine* in 'Pinafore' one week, and played *Juliet* in 'Romeo and Juliet' shortly afterwards. I have appeared in 'Trial by Jury' and 'Othello.' Don't you believe me when I say that my career has been varied?"

Again Miss Ellsler burst into merriment. I had known very little about her earlier life, before she had made her appearance in the metropolis.

"I was to have gone abroad," she went on, "to

study music. Mr. Hess, the manager of the opera company in which I sang, offered to make me his prima donna. But I was afraid of my voice. I had always thought that I was more fitted for a dramatic than an operatic life. Somehow or other I believed that though I might be a very fair singer, I could never attain any great eminence. You see I know my own voice exactly, and dearly as I loved music, I thought it best to give up all idea of singing in opera."

"Then the time you devoted to comic opera, was really time lost," I said.

It was not a very brilliant remark, but I felt that I had to say something to keep up my reputation.

"Not at all," remarked Miss Ellsler. "A knowledge of music is a very great help to actors and actresses, even if they have no designs upon opera. Why, I have known actors who were absolutely unable to vary their tones as a stage manager instructed them to do. They would see no difference between the way he spoke the lines, and the way they spoke them. Their musical education had of course been neglected. Oh, no! I do not look upon the time I devoted to comic opera as lost, by any means."

I was silent, because I thought I might make another wrong suggestion if I spoke.

"Before I came to New York," said Mrs. Weston, "I had the pleasure of playing leading business with Edwin Booth, John McCullough, Lawrence Barrett and others. I first appeared in New York in 'Hazel Kirke,' at the Madison Square Theatre. It was intended that I should play the part of *Dolly*, but for business reasons I played the title role. Steele Mackaye was very pleased. He said that I had been sent to him. I became identified with the part of *Hazel Kirke*. I played it so much that my health broke down at last, and my doctor ordered me rest. But it is strange how thoroughly one becomes identified with a part. On the road my name was hardly remembered, while that of the role I played was in all mouths. A lady in New Orleans was asked if she would like to meet Effie Ellsler. 'Effie Ellsler! who's that?' she demanded. She was told that it was *Hazel Kirke*, and was very anxious to know me."

"Of course you dislike long runs?"

"Indeed I do," replied Miss Ellsler, warmly. "I believe that they make people mechanical. It does an actor or an actress no good to be identified with one part for a long time. Whatever he or she may do afterwards, critics will always find some traces of the long-played role in their work. Then we lose our interest in parts after a certain time—for actors and actresses are extremely human, although the public is inclined to forget that occasionally—and, as soon as the interest is gone, the work becomes purely mechanical. Nothing is worse than a mechanical actor or actress."

Miss Ellsler said that after she left " Hazel

Kirke" she became a star, and has been starring ever since. Now starring is one of my pet subjects. It seems to me such a terrible thing that a talented actor and actress, who would be an acquisition in a city of culture and refinement, should elect to go barnstorming through the country, for the sake of being at the head of an organization, and in a play possessing one strong part for the star, and weak, pitiful roles for everybody else. I tried to say as little as possible on this subject to Miss Ellsler. I have said a great deal about it at times, and written a great deal about it, too. But she understood me very quickly.

"Nobody can say," she declared, "that I appear in one-part plays. I do not believe that any true artist would do it. I am sure that I am anxious for every actor and actress in my company to get as much applause as possible. People require good performances; they want to see every member of the company act well. Oh! I assure you that the public wants the best of everything nowadays. Of course there are one-part plays, in which the star has everything, but I believe the time is coming when such plays will not be tolerated. It is mostly 'specialty' people who are afraid of having good actors and actresses in their companies. I would always rather have my audience leave the theatre and say that they have seen a thoroughly good performance, than find nothing to talk about but Effie Ellsler. There are too many of these specialty people. It seems to me that America's most important theatrical production is the Simon Pure soubrette. The legitimate soubrette has yet to come. Miss Annie Pixley is perhaps the nearest approach to her that we have."

"What kind of work do you prefer for yourself?" I asked.

"I have no preference at all," replied Miss Ellsler, "and I have found that actresses who have passed the greater part of their life on the stage always answer the question in that way. My schooling has been a very thorough one, and it enabled me to do everything—well, at least intelligently. Perhaps I may believe that I am more successful in emotional work, and in the finer comedy roles. But I really always try to avoid thinking this. I am an actress, and it is my duty to play anything. I told you that I had appeared in Shakespearian roles. Can you imagine a tiny little woman like me playing *Rosalind ?* I played all through the country in 'As You Like It,' and was very kindly received. Yes, I am very fond of Shakespeare, but people nowadays seem to hanker for modern plays, and pictures of everyday life. Shakespearian productions are not very successful. The public grows natural. The old stage methods and plays no longer find favor in the eyes of the people. I must say, however, that never has Shakespeare been better played than to-day. He becomes more human, if I may say so, in the hands of our actors and actresses.

His heroes and heroines live with a life far different to the stilted, stereotyped portrayals we used to see.".

Mr. Weston interrupted his wife's interesting discourse at this point, and joined in the conversation. He is a bright, amiable fellow, with a keen eye for business. His career has been about as varied as that of his wife, and he has also sung in comic opera. He is an excellent actor, and his impersonations are always pictures of manly intelligence.

Mr. Weston married into a very pleasant theatrical family, when he became the husband of Miss Effie Ellsler, and he knows it. I am quite sure of that.

MRS. D. P. BOWERS.

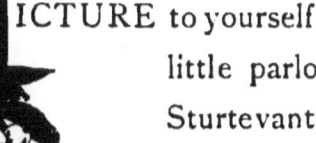

PICTURE to yourself a dainty little parlor in the Sturtevant House, filled with the thousand and one trifles that are dear to the heart of woman, and pleasing to the eye of man. Imagine, in the centre of the pretty things, a sweet-faced, serious-looking lady, with bright, canary-like eyes, and a certain nervousness of manner that compels perpetual attention. That is what I saw when I called upon Mrs. D. P. Bowers, of whom Americans are always proud, and whose name will go down to posterity in the history of the American stage.

Mrs. Bowers is seldom alone. She is generally

surrounded by young people, in whose society she finds a great deal of pleasure. Her parlors in the Sturtevant are very frequently besieged.

Amateurs with dramatic tastes, novices anxious for points, and friends desiring to hear what Mrs. Bowers has to say on the theatrical ques-ions of the day, are always on hand. Mrs. Bowers receives her visitors most charmingly. She is frequently assisted by her friend Miss Courtney Vale, a handsome lady with a commanding presence, and a conversational *finesse* that is very attractive.

I managed to induce Mrs. Bowers to talk about herself, which she is not very fond of doing, strange to say. When she had once begun, however, her subject appeared to interest her.

"The manner in which I came to go upon the stage," she said, "is not so very extraordinary. My brother, Mr. Crocker, was a member of a stock company in New York, and I used to go to see him act. It was my custom to steal away at night, and get into the theatre. No member of my family ever knew I did this. It was my greatest pleasure. The plays I saw used to give me a kind of mental exaltation for which I could never account. After I had returned home I would go straight to my bed-room and recite. I bought plays and read them aloud, and they gave me more pleasure than any novel could possibly have done. The chairs made me a nice audience,—not an enthusiastic one by any means, but one that was politely attentive, and warranted not to interrupt."

I remembered that many actresses upon whose careers "many moons" have beamed, have probably had just such audiences, and not in their own private rooms, but in the theatres in which they were billed.

"One day," continued Mrs. Bowers, "I managed to secure a very old drama, and learned by heart the leading role. I went over it most carefully, and firmly impressed it upon my mind. Then I said to myself, 'Elizabeth, my dear, you shall go upon the stage. I will do all in my power to help you.' With this determination throbbing through my pulses, I set out for the house of an old stage-manager whom I knew— Thomas Barry, by name. He was having tea when I arrived, but, perfectly undaunted, I was shown into the dining-room, which was also the sitting-room and kitchen.

"'What is it you want?' asked Mr. Barry. (I suppose that tea was rather interesting at that moment, and that I was not.)

"'I want to go upon the stage,' I replied with courage. He laughed. His wife looked at me strangely. She evidently thought that I was a queer, old-fashioned looking little thing, and so I undoubtedly was. Mrs. Barry, however, asked her husband why he didn't try me to see what I could do. He thereupon asked me to read the part in the play which I had brought with me. I did this, and he dropped his fork to listen to me. When I had finished he rose and went to an old book-shelf, from which he drew a play entitled 'A Child of Nature.'

"'Now, Miss Crocker,' he said, 'take that home, study the part I have marked, and on Wednesday come with it, letter-perfect, to the theatre.'

" I was thoroughly happy. I walked home on air, said ne'er a word to anybody, but set to work and mastered the part.

" Well, I went to the theatre at the stipulated time, and the first person I met there was my brother. We indulged in a little scene. He was disgusted at me. I was deceitful and sly. I had very little to say, but I was perfectly determined that I would stay where I was.

" Mr. Barry was very cross with me at first, but

it wore off. When I had finished, he patted my head. The members of the company came up to me and spoke kindly, and the leading lady put her arms around me and kissed me. Leading ladies don't do that nowadays."

Mrs. Bowers laughed. No, I was obliged to admit that leading ladies of the present time were by no means given to lavishing embraces on ambitious young novices.

"I was cast for the part I had studied in 'A Child of Nature,'" resumed Mrs. Bowers. "My name, as you know, was Elizabeth Crocker, but I appeared merely as 'a young lady.' I made a success, and I attributed this to the fact that I had absolutely no fear of the public, and, for the matter of that, no fear of anybody in the world. I think that my first night's performance of that part was the best that I ever gave of it. I played that part for five weeks before my name ever appeared upon the programmes. After that I was cast for all kinds of business—boys, soubrettes, and old women. There was nothing that I did not do, and it was a capital school for me. Finally, I became leading lady of the company. Then I went to Philadelphia, where I was known as a full-fledged leading lady. It was in Philadelphia that I made my hit as *Lady Macbeth*. I had a stock company of my own in that city. Philadelphia is very dear to me. It has one of the greenest spots in my memory. Socially and professionally, I was very happy when I was in the Quaker City. I always call it even now my home, though of course it isn't."

Mrs. Bowers sighed, and was silent for a few minutes, which I spent in looking around the pretty, femininely decorated room.

"It was in Philadelphia," she went on, "that I first met Mr. D. P. Bowers, who afterwards became my husband. He was a light comedian. I was very young when I married him. We had three children, who are living. When I am not at the Sturtevant House, and not acting, I am generally visiting my married daughter, who lives in Washington. But—let me see—I am getting too domestic. Where was I?"

She thought for a second, and resumed the lost thread.

"Later," she said, "I went to London, and I shall never forget my English experience, which was a truly delightful one. I appeared at the Lyceum Theatre in 'Peep o' Day,' and played for four hundred nights. Of course I settled down for the time in England. I had a lovely little home in the suburbs, and used to receive my friends on Sunday nights. I met some of the most interesting people on the other side, and among them Charles Dickens. Then I was also introduced to the lady known to the novel-reading public as Ouida. I have heard many people describe her as masculine and unkempt looking. I always thought she was particularly feminine. She dressed in the daintiest manner, and was very fond of woman's little adornments. She said some smart things, and was rather severe upon the men, which rather surprised me, for in her books it is always the women who fare badly, while the men appear as heroes. Millais, the artist, was also one of my acquaintances, but I was not greatly impressed with him. However, I suppose I ought not to be critical. I enjoyed myself very much in England, and took away many charming souvenirs. One of them was a signet ring, which is said to have been worn by Queen Elizabeth, and which I still possess."

I glanced at Mrs. Bowers' hands, but the precious ring did not encircle her finger. Perhaps, I reflected, she used it as a bit of stage property as *Elizabeth.*

"After my London engagement," she said, "I returned to America, and started in on a starring tour, which really lasted for twenty years. I think I can truthfully say so. I have played all over the country. In those days we did not take an entire company with us. The star and the leading man did the travelling, and they were supported by the companies belonging to the theatres at which they played. I think that my greatest successes have been as *Elizabeth* and *Lady Audley*. I made a thorough study of *Elizabeth*. I really felt I was the woman when I was on the stage. I have played with most of the well-known stars,—Forrest, Edwin Booth and Salvini. I was in the great production of 'Othello' at the Metropolitan Opera House, as *Emilia*. My Shakespearian repertoire has also included *Desdemona, Rosalind, Lady Macbeth, Portia*, and other roles."

"And your favorite role?" I asked.

"I love them all," she said. "My career has been one that I can look back upon with pleasure, and it has been full of incidents. When I first appeared in California—I think it was in 1868—E. J. Buckley was in the cast. When I last appeared there, twenty years later, Mr. Buckley's daughter, a young woman, was with me.

She was not born at the time of my first engagement there. It seemed so strange to me, and so pathetic, too. I remember that I made a speech upon that occasion, and I was deeply touched.

"On one occasion in California I had quite an exciting experience. We used to play in the mining camps. One night after playing at one of the camps, I wanted to get to Denver, and could only do so by taking a stage coach. My husband was with me, and we had a great deal of money with us—several thousand dollars, beside valuable jewelry. Just before we started we heard that the coach was to be 'held up,' but as it was only a vague sort of a rumor, we were willing to doubt it. When we took our seats, we found to our dismay that we were the only passengers in the coach. We concealed our money very neatly. It was stitched into our clothes. That ride I shall never forget as long as I live. It was wild and uncanny. The ground was uneven, and we were jolted in a most distressing manner. Suddenly the coach gave a lurch that t was impossible to withstand. We were thrown out. It was pitch dark, but for a moment only. When we arose, we saw three men with lanterns before us. One of them pinioned the driver. The other two devoted themselves to us. I was nearly frightened to death, and so was my husband. We were unarmed, and absolutely in the power of these villains. But an idea occurred to me, and it proved to be a brilliant one. These wretches were looking for Mrs. Bowers. How did they know her? Filled with this idea, I called out to my husband, 'If you had only consented to wait for Mrs. Bowers, we should not have been in this trouble. She is safe, and we——'

"It was a happy thought of mine. The thieves, who had already wended their way into our pockets, and found nothing, seemed to be immediately struck with the force of my remark. With oaths, and murmurs of disgust, they finally told us to get back into the stage, and you can be quite sure the injunction was not disobeyed. When we arrived in Denver, I was ill from the excitement and worry. That awful night will never be forgotten by me."

After the death of Mr. D. P. Bowers, Mrs. Bowers became the wife of James C. McCollom, who is now dead. By him she had no children. During the present season (1890) she has supported Salvini in his farewell American tour.

"I am just as devoted to the stage as ever," she said. "I live for it. When I am away from it I feel as if I must return. It is impossible for me to think of retirement. I always say that when I see the footlights I am like a war horse that scents battle."

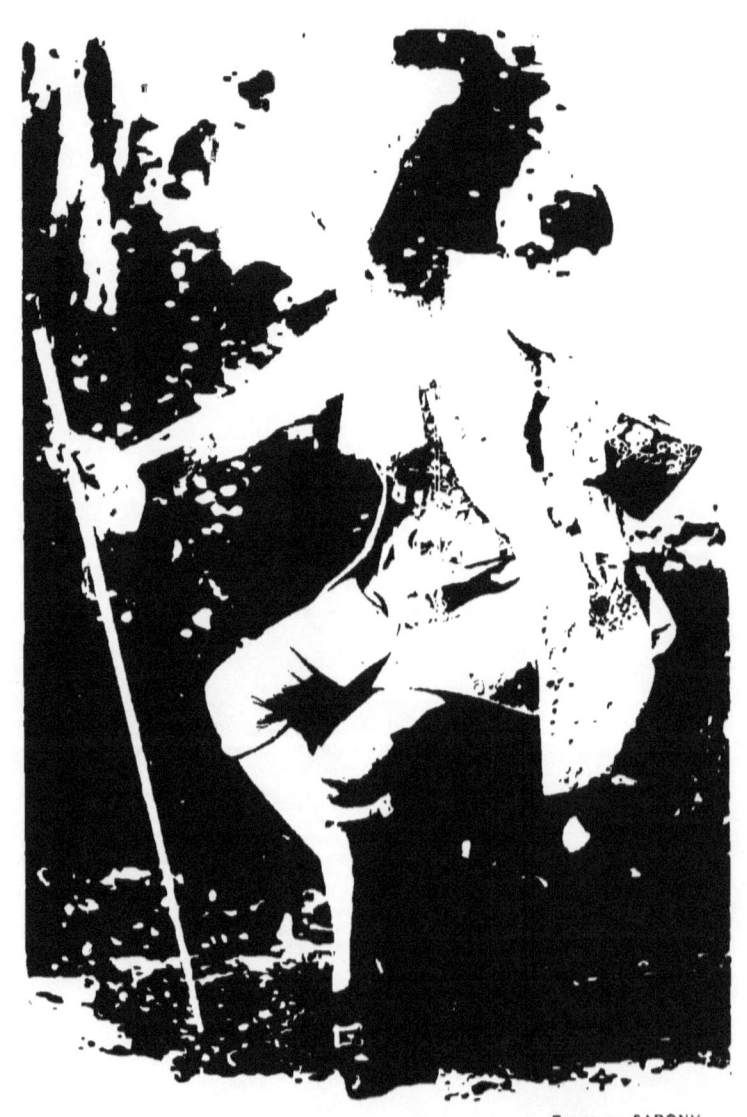

Photo by SARONY.

ADA REHAN.

ADA REHAN.

I BELIEVE it was Pope who defined fame as "a fancied life in others' breath,"—not that it matters much. Every one who thinks about such matters seems to have decided that the joys of fame are hollow, unless they be linked with the more substantial delights of life. The actor who, in his solitary room, reads of the pleasure that he confers upon hundreds of thousands, may be pardoned if, glancing round his silent chamber he wonders why no real pleasure is conferred upon him; the author who sees his books in the market eagerly bought up, looks into the barren reality of his life, and sighs at the will-o'-the-wisp-like quality of fame.

I am about to write a few lines on the subject of Miss Ada Rehan, an actress with whose stage life most of my readers must be tolerably familiar; a woman whose talent has delighted the old world and the new. And I cannot repress the above thoughts when Rehan is in my mind. Her smile which the world sees, does not impress me. There always seems to me to be something wanting.

This grand Rehan lives alone and undisturbed in a handsome flat in Thirty-ninth street. When she leaves the theatre at night, weary and broken, as are most of the hard-worked members of Mr. Daly's company, there are no home voices to cheer her; no gentle, waiting women to distract her thoughts from the channels through which they run so persistently. She has a maid. She has servants. Her flat is luxuriously furnished. She is reported to own it, and all the other flats in the house. But she sees few friends; her life outside of the theatre is a blank. The charming qualities which Ada Rehan undoubtedly possesses are left either to rust or to be used in the fictitious life of the stage. To me, this seems eminently deplorable. Just the same as an author who lives for the creations of his mind must miss the primary objects of life, so must the actor and actress, too, completely enclosed in the pictures behind the footlights, parody the living, breathing man and woman they were intended to represent.

Miss Rehan is the slave of Augustin Daly, and there is no use mincing words in saying so. Daly has made her a great actress. Without him she would probably have never been known, outside of the world of barnstormers. He recognized her talent; he advanced her; he made plays to fit her. She has amply repaid him. To the ambition which he implanted in her bosom, she has sacrificed her life. Yes, I say she has sacrificed her life, and I place all due emphasis on the sacrifice. The world is thankful for this. It has gained everything. In my opinion Ada Rehan is the finest actress of her kind in the world. Beside her, Ellen Terry is insignificant and almost pitiful; compared with her Mme. Jane Hading is worthless.

Wilson Barrett was discussing Ada Rehan a short time ago. Said he: "I have never seen anybody like her. I consider her a genius. It is so easy to detect, in the refinement of her work, the advantages of birth and education."

That is exactly where Mr. Barrett and a great many others fall into grave error. Miss Rehan is a self-educated woman. She was born in Limerick, Ireland, and came to this country when very young, making her first appearance on the stage at the age of fifteen. A very good authority says that she first saw the light of day on the twenty-second day of April, 1859. Augustin Daly, however, has just made out a list setting forth the ages of celebrated people. The list is long. It has been cleverly made to end with the name of Ada Rehan, who, if it is to be believed, was born in 1860. At any rate, Miss Rehan looks a great deal older than she is, and I don't wonder at it. If I were to tell you of the severity of the labor imposed by Mr. Daly upon his people, your hair would stand on end. As somebody has very justly said, he owns their souls and bodies. Not only does he undertake to regulate their conduct while in his theatre, but he permits his rules to haunt them when they have shaken the dust of his house from their feet. When they are tucked up in their little beds at night, he likes them to remember that they are still members of Daly's Theatre.

Miss Rehan is not permitted to speak with newspaper men. None of Daly's people are allowed to do this. They are also prohibited from habitually walking on Broadway in the daytime, as it is the custom of many actors and actresses to do.

Ada Rehan going to rehearsal is really a

remarkable sight. In the first place she dresses execrably. You have seen her on the stage, and have probably been fascinated by the beauty of her costumes. Do you imagine that they were her ideas? Not a bit of it. They emanated from the brain of Augustin Daly. He planned them, he gave them to the dressmaker, he saw that they hung gracefully. In the street Miss Rehan generally wears dark colors. Were she to permit herself the luxury of light shades, I am sure that we should see her in greens, yellows and pinks atrociously combined. Her walk is peculiar. It is hardly a walk. It is a slouch. She looks neither to the right nor to the left. While actresses far less known than Rehan can walk hardly a hundred yards on matutinal Broadway without having to bend their heads in recognition of a score of people, Miss Rehan is unmolested by acquaintances. She belongs to Daly's Theatre. Nobody disturbs her.

I heard an actor one day talking of Rehan in

her girlhood, before Daly had secured her services. She was then playing in a theatre in Albany, and he laughed as he remembered the raw, awkward girl, who seemed more suited to any work than that of the stage. She was accustomed to giggle, and she was fearfully ingenuous and refreshing. Miss Rehan played for two seasons at Mrs. Drew's Theatre in Philadelphia, before she came to Daly's.

The only real pleasure in which Ada Rehan indulges is a visit paid every Sunday to her mother in Brooklyn. To this she looks forward with a great deal of pleasure. She has two sisters, Miss Hattie Russell, who a season ago played with Mrs. Langtry at the Fifth Avenue Theatre, and who resembles Miss Rehan a great deal; and Mrs. Byron, wife of Oliver Doud Byron, the actor. Then she has a brother, Arthur Rehan, a genial, good-natured fellow, who manages what is known as Arthur Rehan's Comedy Company, playing out of town the pieces that Mr. Daly makes known to the metropolis.

As an artist, Miss Rehan has overcome even the prejudices of Londoners. When she first visited England, the apparent affectation of her manner was censured. She is an acquired taste, like olives, and it is only lately that Miss Rehan has been accepted in London at her full worth. The London papers gushed ecstatically over her performance of *Katherine* in "The Taming of the Shrew."

New Yorkers simply adore Rehan. Everything she has done has been applauded. Among her principal successes are roles in "Seven-Twenty-Eight," "Needles and Pins," "The Country Girl," "The Squire," "Love on Crutches," "Nancy and Company," "The Taming of the Shrew," "The Merry Wives of Windsor," and "As You Like It."

Her *Rosalind* is a creditable piece of work. It is being played at the time of this writing. Still it was something of a disappointment. It is by no means the best impersonation that Miss Rehan has given, and everybody seemed to think that her *Rosalind* would be a surprise, another instance, I suppose, of realization falling short of anticipation.

Many people have asked me if I thought that Miss Rehan knew how great an artist she was, her utter want of self-consciousness seeming to warrant the belief that she did not. I cannot help smiling at such refreshingly innocent questions. Just as though any actor or actress that ever lived did not know exactly their standing with the public!

Miss Rehan, believe me, dear reader, charming as she is upon the stage, and fascinating as she certainly can be off the boards, is by no means above the queer little feelings that agitate the profession. She was said to have been fearfully jealous of little Miss Edith Kingdon, now Mrs. George Gould. Miss Kingdon received some favorable notices in Paris, while Miss Rehan was comparatively unnoticed. There was a regular "rumpus," (if you will pardon the apparent slanginess of the expression) in the Daly camp as soon as the notices had been digested. Miss Kingdon was treated rather cruelly, and Mr. Daly took immediate steps to prevent the recurrence of such a frightful catastrophe as the recognition of a member of his company who was not Ada Rehan. It was generally believed that Miss Kingdon's marriage with Mr. Gould was precipitated by the unpleasant results of her success in Paris. And Miss Ada Rehan was credited with being responsible for these unpleasant results.

GEORGIE DREW BARRYMORE.

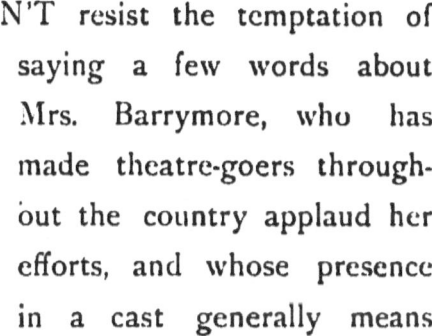

I CAN'T resist the temptation of saying a few words about Mrs. Barrymore, who has made theatre-goers throughout the country applaud her efforts, and whose presence in a cast generally means incessant laughter whenever she is upon the stage. She has recently "stabbed with laughter" those who saw William H. Crane's play, "The Senator," at the Star Theatre. The role of *Mrs. Hillary*, which she assumed in this invigorating comedy, was perhaps one of the best efforts she ever made. Mrs. Barrymore, herself, looked upon it as one of the greatest opportunities she ever had. She certainly made the most of it.

Mrs. Barrymore is as amusing in private life as she is upon the stage. She is a typical American, vivacious, entertaining and irresistible, and in her charming little flat in East Fifty-ninth street, she is one of the most accomplished hostesses imaginable. It is at her home that she prefers to be seen. I wanted a little talk with her about her stage career, and wrote asking when I should call. The following letter is characteristic:

"Will you come up to our flat some night after the theatre, and take supper with Mr. Barrymore and myself? I think it will be so much easier to talk, and you can do more in half-an-hour at that stage of the game with me than in s'teen interviews."

The Barrymores have three lovely little children, of whom they are intensely proud. These children have been the tie that long separations and the distractions of vigorous stage life have been powerless to dissolve. If all husbands and wives. seeking their livelihoods upon the stage, had the same souvenirs of early married life, a pretty home like that possessed by Mr. and Mrs. Barrymore would be less unusual among dramatic couples.

If it is possible to be born dramatic, Georgie Drew must have thought of the green-room while she manipulated her nursing bottle ; she must have anticipated grease-paint when mamma powdered her baby face. She has been surrounded by actors and actresses from the moment she made her first appearance in the world ; she has lived among them ever since.

The Drew family is one of the landmarks of the American stage. Mrs. Barrymore's father was the descendant of a dramatic family, and was himself a clever actor. He was an Irishman, and came to America at an early age. He played his first important engagement in this city, at the Old Bowery Theatre, in 1845, appearing there as *Dr. O'Toole.* He was an Irish comedian, and an interpreter of light comedy roles. Early in the fifties he became manager of the Arch Street Theatre in Philadelphia. He died in 1862 when Georgie was a child, leaving several children, among them John and Sidney.

Mrs. Drew, the mother of this ultra-dramatic trio, is an actress whose praises it is unnecessary to sing. During the present season (1890) she is still acting in support of Messrs. Jefferson and Florence, though the "support" might come as easily from them as from Mrs. Drew. Her *Mrs. Malaprop* in "The Rivals" is simply a joy. Mrs. Drew is an Englishwoman, and played juvenile roles in England before she came to this country. She was first seen in America in 1827, when she was nine years old, as the *Duke of York* to the *Richard III.* of the elder Booth. She is a stately and rather formidable old lady, inclined to dwell, with pardonable pride, upon the immense advantage of being "a Drew." She is very proud of her children, and is generally present at the first performance of any play in which they appear, when her duties do not conflict with such an arrangement. She is very frank in her criticisms, and if her children's work fails to meet with her approval, she is not at all slow in acquainting them with that fact. Mrs. Barrymore can only remember one occasion when her mother succumbed to emotion. She tells the story so funnily that I am almost ashamed to put it into cold print.

A well-known actress of Mrs. Drew's company, now one of the most popular women in New York, (Mrs. Barrymore did not mention names, but I will tell you that I suspect it was Ada Rehan) was playing the part of an Indian girl. She had been ill, and the doctor had ordered her to shave her head, which she had done. Between the acts she sat in her dressing-room without her wig. Her head was white as snow; her face as red as half-a-dozen roses, thanks to the grease-paint she had used rather profusely. Mrs. Barrymore was roaring with laughter at the remarkable spectacle she presented. Mrs. Drew, indignant at the noise, appeared to quell it. She cast one glance at the hairless, painted maiden. The sight was too much for her. "Merciful Heavens!" she cried. Then she fled precipitately.

Mrs. Barrymore's brothers are very popular in this city. John is a member of Mr. Daly's company. He first appeared under the charge of his mamma, of whose teaching the great Augustin Daly must have thought a great deal for he engaged from her theatre, John and

Georgie Drew, and Miss Ada Rehan. Mrs. Barrymore's second brother, Sidney, is also a clever young actor. He redeemed a very bad play called "A Legal Wreck," from much of the contempt that it deserved. Mrs. Barrymore is very interested in her brothers, and justly so. They are clever young men, and owing to their mamma, their opportunities have been many and excellent.

Mrs. Barrymore made her first appearance on the stage when she was seventeen years of age in "The Ladies Battle." She played the youthful role, and her mother that of the countess. Mrs. Drew was not at all anxious that her children should appear upon the stage. Exactly why she should have objected to this is not known. I have generally found, however, that actors and actresses, even the most successsful of them, are very slow in recommending the stage to aspirants. John Drew appeared in direct opposition to his mother's wishes. Mrs.

Barrymore was suffered to appear under protest. But she met with success from the start, and vanquished her mother's objections. She has supported Edwin Booth, John McCullough, Lawrence Barrett, and a number of other celebrated theatrical stars. Mrs. Barrymore now says that she thinks she can understand why her mother was desirous of her following any other career than that of the stage. The public ought to feel thankful that Mrs. Barrymore, like Katisha, had "a will of her own."

Mrs. Barrymore first met her husband, the well-known actor, Maurice Barrymore, while a member of Daly's company, in which organization he also held a position. Barrymore is a delightful fellow to meet. He is an Englishman with a thorough education. He can talk on any subject, and he isn't a bit shoppy. He and his wife are on terms of complete "good-fellowship."

I would like to bet, however, that the three

little Barrymores will never be seen upon the stage. I know nothing at all about it, but I am convinced that Papa Maurice would have a fit at the idea, while Mamma Georgie would indulge in the feminine equivalent—a nice swoon.

LITTLE GERTIE HOMAN.

I HAVE had occasion to write a great deal upon the subject of stage children, whom I have always regarded as well-oiled little machines, speaking their lines and making their gesticulations in the manner prescribed by fond mammas and zealous stage-managers. I have always scouted the idea of these juvenile actors and actresses possessing inherently any of the dramatic "afflatus." I have always wanted to scout this idea, for the notion of an infant, born, as it were, with the power to impersonate somebody else, before it has learned to interpret its own mission in life, is somewhat repulsive. I must confess, however, that I felt inclined (only inclined, mind you) to waver in my views after my visit to sweet little Gertie Homan the other day. This dainty little maiden, who made such an immense success in

"Partners," "The Burglar," and "Bootle's Baby" at the Madison Square Theatre, and in "Little Lord Fauntleroy" out of town, is simply just as much of a surprise off, as upon the stage.

Gertie lives with her homely, unpretentious parents in a neat flat at No. 452 Wythe avenue, Williamsburg, and it was there that I saw her a few mornings ago. The little maiden was waiting for me at the top of the stairs. Such a fragile, winsome little thing! She wore a red dress, and her dark, fluffy hair made an ebon halo around her rather pallid face, which was lighted by a pair of the most lustrous eyes I have ever seen.

"Mr. Dale?" she queried, in a perfectly self-possessed manner, as she shook my hand (she isn't eight years old yet) and led the way into the room.

I followed the child, and we entered a plainly furnished but tasteful little parlor.

Gertie had a doll almost as large as herself in her arms, and she seemed to be extremely proud of it.

"I have thirty dolls," she said gleefully. "Love them? I just kiss them all day long when I am at liberty."

At liberty! The regular stage expression from the mouth of this mite!

I sat down opposite her, and she introduced me to her father, a gray-haired, amiable old man, whose tongue seemed to be singularly inactive. I wanted to hear something about this child, whom I have always admired, but I wondered how I could hear it from this silent papa. I did not imagine that the child herself would know how to tell her story. I made a very great mistake.

"I'm not acting now," she said demurely, seeming to divine my embarrassment. "Mamma thought I needed a rest. I didn't. I am so fond of acting, and have hardly had a day idle in a year. It isn't work for me, Mr. Dale."

She spoke with the assurance of a woman. I felt that my embarrassment was so ridiculous in the presence of this matter-of-fact young lady, that I made a great effort, and resolved to talk to her just as though she were full-fledged.

"And you find no trouble in learning such long parts?"

"Oh, none at all," with surprise, "I can learn a part in two days. I got 'Little Lord Fauntleroy'—let me see" (meditatively) "one Saturday, and I had to play it the following week. That part, you know" (very solemnly) "is as long as 'Hamlet.' But my favorite part was the little girl in 'Partners.' I thought it very sweet and very sympathetic" (these were her own words, I assure you). "I had a great deal of crying to do, and I liked it so much."

"She is very fond of stage crying," put in the father, with a fond glance at little Miss Pertness.

"Then," she went on, not heeding papa's interruption, "I liked the part of *Editha* in 'The Burglar.' Editha was an awfully nice child—a cunning little thing, you know. In 'Bootle's Baby,' *Mignon* was really very like myself—more like myself than any other parts I have played. So it wasn't at all difficult."

Miss Homan stroked her doll's flaxen hair with maternal hands, and sat bolt upright in her chair. She was evidently enjoying herself. I felt that if I didn't hurry on, she would interview *me*. I saw the desire in her eyes.

"Is Gertie your only daughter, Mr. Homan?" I asked.

Gertie laughed. "Papa had ten children," she said, before he could answer, "and I am the youngest. There are seven living. Come and see the picture of five of us taken together."

Mr. Homan brought me the photograph in question. No wonder that he looked proudly upon it. Five comely girls in a group, and all his own daughters! Gertie was among them, the prettiest of the lot. I believe that the mite knew this, too. Mrs. Homan and her daughter Lulu entered the room as I was lost in admiration of the pretty domestic photograph. Mrs. Homan is a foreigner, with a face not unlike that of Mme. Modjeska. She was born in Dresden, and educated in Paris. The coarse black dress, and the plain white apron she wore could not conceal her charming dignity, and the intrinsic refinement of her manner. I always think that the most delightful being on earth is a motherly mother. Such was Mrs. Homan. She beamed upon Gertie and upon Lulu, and it wasn't done for effect, either, as I was very quick to perceive. I have mixed too much with theatrical people to be easily taken in.

Mrs. Homan told me that she was a relative

of Charles Schiller, a writer living in Paris. She had been in this country a number of years.

"We settled in New Orleans," she said, "and it was there that Gertie, at the age of three years, recited for Sunday School entertainments. She made such a hit that a gentleman in New Orleans said to me, 'If you don't take that child, and put her on the stage, it will be a sin!' Gertie was born in New Orleans, within a half mile of where Jefferson Davis lived. Well, we came on to New York, and were lucky at the very beginning. The only trouble I seemed to find was that Gertie was too perfect for some of the juvenile parts—too perfect to be natural. But it was a very satisfactory fault, and it never stood in her way. She has never had one day's sickness. I have never had a doctor for her. She is a thoroughly healthy child."

Gertie listened to her mother in a condescending way. She had settled herself upon the lap of Miss Lulu, a pleasing girl of about seventeen years of age, who fondled her little sister as though she were a doll.

"Gertie gets along so admirably with the people in the companies with which she plays," continued the fond mamma.

"I love Miss Burroughs, of the Madison Square," interrupted Gertie, eagerly. "She is so pretty, and so amiable. And as for young Mr. Salvini, I like him well enough to marry him. There, now!"

Miss Lulu laughed reprovingly.

"I have been advised to keep the child on the stage until she is thirteen years old," resumed Mrs. Homan. "I went to Mr. A. M. Palmer and asked for his advice. 'By all means, Mrs. Homan,' said he. 'Keep her on the stage.' When she is thirteen, I intend to send her to Paris, and let her remain there until she is nineteen."

"Oh, dear!"—from Gertie.

"I believe in giving her a thorough education.

It is just as necessary, and even more necessary for the stage than for other walks in life."

"Do you teach Gertie her parts?" I asked.

"Sometimes I, and sometimes Lulu," replied Mrs. Homan. "She is very quick to learn them."

"Indeed she is," said Miss Lulu, "and she understands them, too. I say to her, 'Now, Gertie, suppose you were that little girl. How would you say those words?' She immediately answers, 'I would say them like this, or like that,' and she generally strikes the right method. I think that is the very best way to teach children. It is an appeal to themselves, and they rarely forget what they have been taught in a reasonable manner. Very often Gertie needs no instruction in gesticulation at all. It really seems to come quite naturally to her."

"I don't like my child to leave New York," said Mrs. Homan, "but she has been obliged to go out of town with companies. Lulu traveled with her. Gertie got a weekly salary of eighty dollars, and all expenses paid. I put all her money aside for her education. Next season I think I shall travel with her myself."

"Are any of your other daughters on the stage?" I asked.

"No; Lulu played a few nights in 'Bootle's Baby,' as *Humpy*, *Mignon's* nurse. But my children, though not upon the stage," she added proudly, "are all clever. Lulu has done a great deal of writing—"

"Oh, mamma!"—from the bashful Lulu—"and one of my daughters draws and paints beautifully. All those pictures" (pointing to some very pretty sketches on the wall) "were done by her. I have a daughter who is cashier in a large clothing establishment. Oh! I assure you that my children are clever. I call them my jewels. They are all I have."

Mrs. Homan showed me a handsome book presented to Gertie by the members of the

Madison Square Theatre company when Gertie left that organization. It contained the signatures of all the actors and actresses who had played with her.

Then Gertie dragged me off to see her playroom, situated at the other end of the flat. It was a large, light apartment. At one end was a bookcase, of the two lower shelves of which Gertie had made a doll's house. She had divided each shelf into two roomlets, which she had carpeted and furnished.

Then she had a large kitchen, with a real stove in it.

"See," she said, "I can put on coal, and dump my fire, and rake it, and cook beautiful things."

I was glad to see that she could be genuinely amused with the toys that please children of her age. Above her stove was a picture of little Miss Elsie Leslie, another child actress.

"You like Miss Leslie?" I asked, a little curiously.

"I think she is beautiful," replied Gertie readily, "I always keep her picture in my kitchen. I met her once at a reception given to stage children, and I fell in love with her. I have seen her act, and I think she acts splendidly."

That sounded nice. I liked to hear it. I looked into the large, honest eyes of the child and could not doubt her possession of a sweet, lovable disposition, that contact with the stage had in no way harmed. I was charmed with the Homans—mother, father, Lulu and Gertie.

"Are you going so soon?" asked Gertie regretfully, as I rose to leave.

And I shouldn't have been human, if I had not liked her all the better for that little bit of interrogation.

LILLY POST.

LILLY POST is in private life Mrs. William H. Morton. Her husband was formerly manager of the Columbia Theatre in Chicago, and is a very energetic gentleman. It is rarely that a comic opera prima donna has a theatrical husband of such good standing as Mr. Morton. The husband of the prima donna is, as a rule, a gentleman with a superb scorn for hard work; one of those amiable, fragrant creatures, who look upon "wifey" with admiring eyes, and are very glad indeed that she is so popular with the public. But Mr. Morton is not one of those conjugal hangers-on. If Miss Post were to retire, I rather imagine that Mr. Morton would interpose no objections.

When I called upon Miss Post at the Hotel Vendome, she kept me waiting so long in the parlors of the hotel that I began to imagine that she was going to be very ceremonious. I am

always suspicious of a doctor who permits a patient to sit for hours in an ante-chamber, unless this doctor be somebody of national reputation. I would never pin my faith to a lawyer who adopts this policy, because I know it to be one of the tricks of the trade. With a comic opera singer or an actress, there is very fre_ quently a tendency to affect the procession of callers, each waiting impatiently for his little five minutes.

So I began to believe that I was not going to

like *la* Post. I had never met her, though I had frequently heard her sing, and admired that fresh, pure voice, which seems almost too good for a comic opera singer. Just as I was on the verge of the fidgets, a portière was swept aside, and a lady with an extended hand stood before me. I at once recognized Miss Lilly Post, though I was bound to admit that it was difficult to do so. Mrs. W. H. Morton is a very different woman to Miss Lilly Post. The former is majestic and portly; the latter arch and inclined to be kittenish. The matron is simple and rather timid; the singer is vivacious and conspicuous. I no longer wondered at the delay to which I had been subjected. It was before noon, but Miss Post was absolutely resplendent. She wore a costume that nothing on earth could ever induce me to attempt to describe. It was brown in many shades, and it was befrilled and befurbelowed, and bewildering. Diamonds of purest ray serene glistened in Miss Post's dainty ears.

"I am sure I have nothing to say about myself," began my fair hostess, with genuine modesty. "It is quite a new experience for me to talk about Miss Post. What is there to tell? Really I do not know."

I convinced the winsome *Yum-Yum* that her career was surely interesting, as is that of every woman who has succeeded—by which I do not mean to infer that those who have not discovered success could not be even more entertaining and instructive to the public. But people prefer to hear about success, because it generally means merit, though lack of success does not always signify want of merit.

"I was originally," she began, "a church singer. I used to lend my soprano tones regularly to church services in San Francisco, where I was born, and I had no more intention of ever appearing before the public in comic opera than you have yourself at the present moment." (Miss Post could have used no more emphatic argument, as far as I was concerned.) "My appearance was purely accidental. I was one of the numerous 'Pinafore' débutantes. A single performance of this charming little opera was given, and the manager was hunting for a *Josephine*. My position as the church soprano was rather a prominent one, and he happened to think of me. He broached the subject to me, and though my people were fearfully opposed to any such thing, I consented to appear, and did appear as *Josephine*. After that I sang the role at the Bush Street Theatre in San Francisco with the Emily Melville company. That is how I happened to go upon the stage. Not a single member of my family had ever been theatrical. Indeed, my father was a very quiet, unassuming citizen of San Francisco, and in a bank in that city. Since I have been before the public, a younger brother emulated my example, and went upon the stage."

Miss Post was beginning to see that she could be interesting. It is astonishing how appetizingly a career can be dished up, with a little care.

"I came east with the Emily Melville company," resumed Miss Post, "and when it was combined with the McCaull opera company, I was there at the consolidation. The organization was known as the 'McCaull Comic Opera Company,' and with it I remained for six years. I sang in all the operas that McCaull produced. Since I left the company I have been roaming around, so to speak. Of late I sang with the Henderson company in 'The Gondoliers,' and I am now with Mr. Duff. Yes, I like the life very much, but comic opera was not the goal of my ambition."

Miss Post laughed, and I knew what was coming.

"I had great thoughts of grand opera," she said, laughing, "I had a repertoire of ten operas. Think of that! You know I have really worked very hard with my voice. I studied in Paris for a short time, and when I returned to this country, I continued to labor very assiduously. In

San Francisco I had the very best musical cultivation that money could purchase. One of my teachers had been a pupil of the celebrated Mme. Marchesi in Paris. Have I given up all thoughts of grand opera? Well, perhaps I had better say that I have."

Miss Post said this with such charming candor, and her manner was so unconventional and free from restraint, that I mentally begged her pardon, and wondered how I could possibly have dreamed of ceremony in her connection.

"I practice every day," said Miss Post, "and when you came, I was exercising my voice. That is why I am hoarse at the present time." (She wasn't.) "When I neglect practising, I never sing so well at night, as I have discovered to my cost. Opera singers should never go upon the stage unless they have previously gone over the scales. No matter how short the exercise may be, practice is absolutely necessary. If only ten minutes each day can be spared, those ten minutes will be very valuable. I used to stay at a hotel where Herr Fischer, the German singer, whom you have undoubtedly heard at the Metropolitan Opera House, with his wife, used to occupy rooms directly beneath mine. Every morning I used to hear him arise, and before he could possibly have time to dress, he would go to the piano and run over the scales."

I ventured to remark that, in Miss Post's place, I should have selected another part of the hotel.

"But he was most considerate," she resumed, laughing. "He always sang *pianissimo*, and I was very much interested. What Fischer did was much better than all the absurd preparations and voice tonics that singers take before appearing upon the stage. I used to imagine that I couldn't possibly sing unless I drank a glass of sherry, or ate a raw egg. This is utter nonsense. Some people, I believe, even drink a glass of sweet oil, and this, it seems to me, is really injurious. Oil will clog up the throat, unless the singer happens to have a cold. Only in that case will it possibly prove beneficial. Just before appearing, the very best thing to do is to exercise the glottis. Teachers of professional singers give them an exercise by which they can work the glottis without uttering a tone, just as pianists with a silent piano can exercise their fingers without producing a sound. Sometimes I take a little bit of rock candy, and that is positively the extent of my vocal preparations."

"You have never appeared in anything but comic opera?" I asked.

She smiled.

"I am a little ashamed to say," she replied, "that I played in the burlesque extravaganza known as 'Bluebeard, Jr.' I was doing nothing, and I thought I might as well do this in Chicago. The costumes were lovely, and my role was a nice one, but I don't care to think about it too much, you know. You may have discovered that I am just as ambitious now as I ever was. I thought, when I married Mr. Morton, that I would give up the stage, and settle down into a nice, quiet, domestic wife. I tried it, and I found" (Miss Post made a queer little wry mouth) "that I could not possibly give up my lovely stage. Life seemed too tame without it. There was no aim in anything. I might even have gone back to church singing, and made a great deal of money by it, too. But I had scented comic opera, and I had found it to be positively irresistible. There is something about the fascination of the stage that I am utterly unable to explain. I only know that it exists. What it is, and why it is, I have never been fortunate enough to discover, though I have attempted to analyze myself and my motives. There is a something—a *je-ne-sais-quoi*, as the French say, that defies description Since we have been married, Mr. Morton and I have lived in Chicago. He tells me that there is a possibility of Denver in the future, and I rather dread the idea of it."

Miss Post has sung a great deal in the comic operas of Gilbert and Sullivan. She is extremely fond of Sir Arthur's music. One of the roles upon which she looks favorably is that of *Mabel* in " The Pirates of Penzance," as she considers that in its florid music she has opportunities for vocal efforts. She has lately been singing the part of *Yum-Yum* in " The Mikado " at the Broadway Theatre, and she is not at all fond of the part. Miss Post prides herself upon her high notes, and is never thoroughly happy unless she can bring them into play. She has all the physical development of the successful opera singer, and I think that she could very advantageously attempt roles of a more arduous nature than those with which she has been identified.

Miss Post is no longer a pet of those connoisseurs of comic opera success, known as the gilded youth. There was a time when the dear chappies used to drop in for an hour, don't you know, to hear the Post. That was at the time when she was singing in "The Black Hussar," with the McCaull Comic Opera company. • Since she became Mrs. Morton, Miss Post has been cruel enough to desert the metropolis, comparatively speaking, and to devote herself to the financially interesting, but by no means artistically appreciative West. Her interests, of course, are there.

Miss Post's photographs are not at all kind to her. In fact, they treat her rather cruelly, accentuating the peculiar lines of her mouth, which is her least desirable feature. She is a very comely woman, with pretty light hair and eyes, and a clear white complexion.

ELLEN GERRY.

ELLEN TERRY.

HE big steamship, Fulda, had just steamed into Quarantine with an unusually large freight of sea-weary passengers, who flocked to the rail that surrounded the deck and gazed eagerly at the signs of busy humanity, as a welcome picture relieving an ocean-tossed condition of chaos.

Hardly had the Fulda cast a temporary anchor, than a little yacht, upon which were a number of city people, including your humble servant, approached. A tall, lank being and his companion, a sunny-haired, smiling woman, were distinctly visible, uttering farewells to the Fulda's passengers, and preparing to descend a flight of steps leading from the imposing vessel to the comparatively ridiculous yacht.

The lank individual was Henry Irving, stately even after his sea voyage; classical after the utter prose of the transatlantic crossing. His companion was of course Miss Ellen Terry, as supremely charming as though she had just stepped from her London home. They were soon on board the yacht, regretfully watched by the less-welcomed passengers.

Miss Terry became emotional as soon as we had started for the city. A tear or two lurked in her eyes, and she talked rather wistfully of home. I imagined that this was a little bit of affectation, devised to please the newspaper men, who were watching her every movement with lynx eyes. I was mistaken, and learned later that Miss Terry, in her private life, is as emotional as in any of the roles she is called upon to portray.

That was the first glimpse I had of her—on board that little yacht. She talked very charmingly, but very informally, and when not thus engaged, devoted herself to her little daughter, Edith Wardell, who accompanied her.

I say "little daughter." Perhaps, however, I am unnecessarily gallant. Miss Terry is one of the few actresses who "make no bones" about telling their ages. While in this country, she celebrated her fortieth birthday, the year of her birth being 1848. So, under the circumstances, I will tell the truth, and say Edith Wardell, when I first saw her, was a great, big, awkward girl, with a rather incongruous assumption of juvenility. She was evidently very proud of "mamma," and rarely budged from her side.

Miss Wardell is not at all pretty. She certainly betrays little resemblance to her lovely mother, which induces the inference that Wardell, himself, could not have been a beauty. I believe he was an artist, and that he died recently.

Miss Terry always treats Irving with great respect. On one occasion, speaking of him to an American, she said: "I look upon him as a god." In fact, there is a sort of mutual admiration society between these two artists. Irving never loses an opportunity of praising Miss Terry, and in nearly all his speeches allusions are made to "that charming actress, Miss Ellen Terry, whom you have all admired."

I had the felicity of accompanying Mr. Irving and Miss Terry to West Point when they played "The Merchant of Venice," without scenery, at the Military Academy. It was an occasion I shall never forget, so completely different to the prosaic everydayness of things. I have seldom seen such genuine pleasure shown by a human being as that manifested by Ellen Terry. The applause of the cadets seemed to afford her the keenest delight. After the performance she held a little court of her own. She was literally an island surrounded by cadets. They asked her questions, she answered them gladly, and if all those boys didn't melt beneath the warmth of those Terry smiles, lavished upon them with a reckless disregard of the adult visitors who were comparatively out in the cold—well, I am no judge.

"I hate to leave West Point," said Miss Terry, as she stepped into the sleigh that was waiting to convey the party from the academy to the railway station. "Those dear boys! That is the sweetest audience to which I have ever played."

Miss Terry is something of a "dowdy" in her attire, when not on the stage. I met her at some private theatricals given in aid of the Neighborhood Guild, and at which her daughter Edith played. I was rather astonished at her dress, which was of the style popularly known as "Susan's Sunday out." Let me see if I can recall it. She wore a dark green silk, as old-fashioned as the hills, and it was made in an ancient, unlovely style. In fact, if I recollect rightly, she wore a "panier," an article which I believe was the rage when Mr. and Mrs. Noah walked into the ark.

But Miss Terry's sun-kissed tresses (though I am not at all sure that they are golden by means of the sun) and her clear-cut cameo face, called all glances very quickly away from her dress. With such personality, anybody could afford to disregard the sartorial question.

I might here say that Miss Wardell certainly showed none of her mother's dramatic talent. I believe the occasion to which I have referred was the first time that the young girl had played a speaking part. She had appeared as witches and fairies in the production of "Faust." Miss Terry has a son, who was educated at Heidelberg, and who has lately appeared with her in London, in "The Dead Heart," at the Lyceum, if I am not mistaken.

And now just a word about the career of this

actress, who has defied criticism by her naturalness, and absolute absence of all self-consciousness. She first appeared in 1856. That sounds fearfully long ago, doesn't it? But I must hasten to remark that, at the time, Miss Terry was but eight years of age. She played the part of *Mamilius* in "The Winter's Tale," at the time when Kean was managing the Princess Theatre, London. Two years later she appeared as *Arthur*, in what we now call "a great production" of "King John."

It is a mistake to suppose that Miss Terry was unknown before Mr. Irving engaged her. She made a distinct success in 1863, when she appeared at the Haymarket Theatre with Sothern in "The Little Treasure;" in 1867 as *Rose de Beaurepaire* in "The Double Marriage;" and in 1874 as *Susan Morton*, in "It Is Never Too Late to Mend." Miss Terry, at the opening of the Lyceum Theatre by Henry Irving, December 30, 1878, appeared as *Ophelia* to the *Hamlet* of Mr. Irving. She was certainly recognized as an artist of purest ray, and since that time nobody has been able to dethrone her. Ellen Terry is more natural on than off the stage, if I may be indulged with such a paradox. The effervescent girlishness, the spontaneous good-humor, and the delicate bits of "business" that she introduces into her roles, are unrivalled in their excellence. In my opinion, she is at her best as *Beatrice* in "Much Ado About Nothing."

Clara Morris.

HERE have been few actresses who have been more discussed and analyzed in their day than Miss Clara Morris, the "queen of emotion;" few actresses have enjoyed a more brilliant and more successful day. If Miss Morris were to retire at the present time, she would do so in comparatively unrivalled glory. The indications, however, are that she will play herself into old age, struggle with those odious comparisons, which, miasma-like, are beginning to arise, and end in the sorrowful way made known by the great Ristori, who returned to America for a last tour, to ruin a perfect fortification of illusion.

Of one thing I am deeply regretful. It is that I never saw Clara Morris at her greatest; when the American people raved about the sublimity of her emotional work and listened eagerly to countless stories of her studies in mad-houses, of her nocturnal visits to hospitals and dissecting rooms, and to various other little tales as profitable as they were interesting. I saw Clara Morris within the last five years, and set her down as the "queen of spasms." The electrical effect of her work is undoubtedly as forcible as it ever was; she can still thrill an audience with the absolute reality of her emotion; the women can yet weep, as they look at Miss Morris' eyes, into which the real wet tears well so genuinely, but save for these spasms, I must confess that Miss Morris was to me a grievous disappointment. In her quieter moments, she appeared crude and unrefined, and there were times when I could quite understand the feelings of those who portrayed her as "wildly western."

But in spite of all her faults, Clara Morris is a case of genius, and her name in the annals of the American stage is luminous for all time.

Miss Morris has won her fame amid obstacles that in the present state of the drama, when pretty faces and handsome forms are looked upon as unquestioned passports to success, would seem unconquerable. She has a face that is far from beautiful, and a figure that is gaunt and unlovely. I always think of Gilbert and that " left shoulder blade, which is a miracle of loveliness," when I see Clara Morris. I do hope that she possesses this boon, even if we are never to know the truth for ourselves. She looks like a thoroughly healthy, robust woman, and it requires the most vivid imagination to give credence to the stories of her ineffably exhausted state, her broken nerves, her need of drugs, and other requirements.

It would be awful to believe that so great an artist would have recourse to feeble fiction. When, however, one sits for half an hour in utter impatience between every act of a performance, to be told that Miss Morris' nerves need attending to, the inner self talks unkindly.

Actresses, strange to say, love to give the impression that they feel the griefs they portray so intensely, that it affects their domestic life. Sarah Bernhardt would have a fit if you dared to suggest health to her. Only the other day I read of her intense suffering, during which she sat up in bed, in a white satin night-gown, her hair in picturesque confusion, and her room filled with artists, who took turns sitting by her bedside. Think of the intense suffering that will permit such obtrusive idiocy; picture the tortured frame in the white satin frills, or the throbbing head with the Psyche knot!

Miss Clara Morris is very much in this style. When a newspaper man asks her if she is well, this is a specimen reply:

'"Well, did you say? Yes, for me; but not perfectly well. I never expect to be that in this world. Perhaps when I get to a better, with a good many other people, I may enjoy perfect health for the first time."

Now, Miss Morris is one of those women who thoroughly enjoy this wicked world. Why it should make her ill, I can't make out. She has a devoted husband, F. C. Harriott, and a lovely home at Riverdale-on-the-Hudson. When she is not acting, she is placidly enjoying herself. She is an accomplished equestrienne, and is a well-known figure, on horseback, in the leafy lanes of Riverdale. Supreme health seems to hover around her. Isn't it funny that these stage people can't be absolutely natural off the stage? Is it not equally ludicrous that perfect health, God's most lovely gift, should be looked upon as unromantic, prosaic, detrimental to success? Our consumptive Sarah, and our nerve-racked Clara are peculiar instances of those idols the people love to worship. Sarah's tuberculosis is a dainty little recognition of the requirements of her supporters; Clara's nerves have made a fortune all by themselves.

Miss Morris was born at Morristown, Canada, in 1848, and began her stage career in Cleveland, in 1862.

"I was living in Cleveland," said Miss Morris, "and there boarded in the same house with my mother, a Mrs. Bradshaw, an actress, and her daughter Blanche. John Ellsler produced 'The Seven Ravens,' and Blanche had a place in the ballet. She worried my mother to let me join her, and made my mother's life miserable until she gained her consent. Blanche took me down to the theatre, but Mr. Ellsler said I was too little, and that unless he could find somebody to march with me, he could not give me a place. I burst into tears. John Ellsler seemed to be sorry for me. He patted me on the head, and told me to come to the theatre. He secured an old-fashioned little woman to walk with me, and everything went well. I appeared as a fairy, and a very strange fairy I looked. After that I was a zouave, and went on the stage in boy's clothes. Blanche and I used to chew gum, and it didn't seem to interfere with our acting. 'The Seven Ravens' ran for two weeks, and my salary was $3 per week. Mr. Ellsler asked me if I would remain with him the following season. My mother refused his request at first, but finally gave her consent, saying that I might as well do this as anything else. That is how I came to go upon the stage."

Miss Morris lived in Cleveland for a number of years, and appeared in Buffalo in 1866. She also played in Cincinnati, where for one season she occupied the position of leading lady, at a salary of $35 per week. She supported her mother, and, as may be imagined, was not able to enjoy a very luxurious life. Her local reputation as an actress was excellent, but actresses don't care very much for local reputations, unless the locality be the metropolis. Miss Morris, however, received some very good offers, one from Augustin Daly, of New York city. She packed up her trunk, bade a temporary good-bye to her mother, and set out for the metropolis, at her own expense.

When Miss Morris first came to New York, she had in her pocket a contract with Mr. Maguire, of California. He pledged himself to give her $100 per week "in gold," two benefits, and the right to choose her own parts as leading lady. But Miss Morris sighed for New York; it was the Mecca of her hopes. She had but two dresses in the world, and a very meagre stage wardrobe. She possessed none of those sartorial "dreams" that actresses of the present day seem to consider as necessary as dramatic talent. Talking of dresses reminds me that on one occasion I had to criticise a feminine star who was playing the part of a governess. To my astonishment, she appeared in the most gorgeous gowns, Worth-made and exceedingly costly. I mentioned the incongruity of a governess donning such garbs. This was her reply:

"I know they are gorgeous, but if I appear out of town in cheap clothes, people will say that I am not a success, and am unable to wear startling dresses. I have got to make an 'appearance.'"

This, by-the-way, of course.

Miss Morris describes her own appearance when she presented herself before the austere Augustin Daly for the first time, as follows:

"Mr. Daly had been accustomed to the magnificence of Miss Morant, Fanny Davenport, Agnes Ethel, and others of his splendid stock company. He looked down upon my five feet three inches, clad in a rusty linen gown, and carrying a satchel. He shrugged his shoulders, and there was doubt expressed in every line of his face. He engaged me to play any part save that of soubrette and general utility. My salary was to be $40 per week, with the understanding that if I made a distinct hit, it was to be doubled. Upon this sum I was to live, support my mother, and buy my stage dresses."

Miss Morris declares that when she had brought her mother to New York, and settled down, she had not one dollar to her credit. Mother and daughter were so cramped for means, that meat once a day was a luxury. The young actress was often so weak at rehearsal, that she was unable to do herself justice. Her mother used to ask if she would have her chops to rehearse upon or to act upon. Miss Morris often used to think that in those days Daly was convinced that she would make a fearful *fiasco*. She suffered very acutely herself. Her stage wardrobe was no use at all for the modern society plays in which she was called to appear, while the tortures of shabbiness were felt when she mingled at rehearsal with the beautifully dressed women of the company.

Miss Morris met with her first metropolitan

triumph through the usual accidents. In theatrical life, accidents are very frequently blessings. Mr. Daly was to present "Man and Wife," a dramatization of Wilkie Collins' famous novel. Miss Agnes Ethel was cast for the part of *Anne Sylvester;* Miss Morris was to appear as *Blanche*, a comparatively insignificant role. At the last moment Miss Ethel refused to act, with the charming caprice of the successful actress. Miss Morris received the part, and was told that she would be required to play *Anne Sylvester* that night. She did so unhesitatingly. It is in just this way that dramatic reputations are made. Her *Anne Sylvester* was a triumph. She was called five times before the curtain on the opening night. Her metropolitan reputation was established.

Miss Morris has made her principal successes as *Camille*, as *Mercy Merrick* in "The New Magdalen," as *Cora* in "Article 47," as *Alixe* and as *Renée de Moray*.

Her *Camille* has always attracted a great deal of attention. The death scene is a wonderful piece of work. Miss Morris has always disliked the part, and declares that she never really intended to play it. She first appeared as Dumas' consumptive heroine very unwillingly. She had just returned to New York after a long absence, to find that the theatres had decided upon giving an entertainment for the benefit of the poor. The winter had been a hard one, and the distress in New York, in the tenement districts, had been very great. Miss Morris consented to appear, and a list of parts was given to her to select from. It was headed by *Camille*, through which she immediately drew a pencil. Her wish was disregarded. A couple of days before the performance she found that she must appear as *Camille*, or remain out of the programme.

Miss Morris made the best of matters, and studied the objectionable role. There was but

-one rehearsal, and Frank Mayo, well known now in connection with "Nordeck" and "Davy Crockett," was the *Armand Duval.* The fateful night arrived, as fateful nights have a way of doing. Miss Morris selected her dresses with a great deal of care. Her manager was having scenery painted for a new French play that he was to produce. It was never produced. "Camille" was a gigantic success, and Miss Morris found the part foisted upon her.

She then made it a special study. " I learned from my physician," she said upon one occasion, "that there are two coughs peculiar to lingering consumption. One of them is a little hacking cough that interferes with the speech, and injures the throat ; the other is a paroxysm brought on by extra exertion. I chose the paroxysm, and introduced it in the first scene, after I have been dancing. *Camille* says at one time that all pain is gone. My doctor told me that this was on account of entire loss of the lungs. He cautioned me against saying much after that, and told me that the tubes of the throat could be used for a few words. I studied *Camille* in this manner, and not in the coarse way that has been attributed to me."

A great deal of nonsense has been written on the subject of Miss Morris' ideas. Probably but very little of it emanated from the artist herself. The St. Louis *Post Despatch* printed a very interesting account of Miss Morris' views on emotion, and as her manager has had the talk printed for circulation, it is worth giving in part:

"You cannot affect other people except by feeling yourself," she said. "You must feel, or all the pretty and pathetic language in the world won't make people sympathize with you. You must cry yourself, and tears alone won't do it. There must be tears in your voice, in order to bring them forth from other people. Before I appear on the stage, I am in a nervous tremor, all because I am afraid that I shan't cry in the play. I spend an hour or two with my company, making just as much fun as I possibly can, so as to get all the laughter out of me. Then I shut myself up, and work up an artificial agony. To do this, I think of some sad incident, or read a sad story. One of Bret Harte's books supplied me with emotion for two years.

"I get the story fixed in my mind, and dwell upon the most pathetic incident in it until my feelings are completely aroused. Then I cry, and the whole thing is done. I have to look out for the other danger, and keep from being overcome. All the false sobs in the world will never take the place of real emotion. There must be real tears in eyes or voice. This is very hard on the eyes, of course. Mine are sometimes so inflamed that I can scarcely use them. We cannot play emotional scenes as they were formerly played. It used to be that there was only one way of dying on the stage. All that has been changed."

Clara Morris is an ardent admirer of Sarah Bernhardt. "Her *Camille* is perfect," she said on one occasion. "She has a wonderful voice, that thrills her audiences, but she does not make you cry. She is a supreme artist. I went to see her in 'Adrienne Lecouvreur,' and was beginning to be deeply moved. But the crisis came too quickly. The large audience was waiting in pained expectancy. I leaned forward and listened. Every word fell upon my ear. I was harrowing rapidly, when—she cleared her throat. The spell was broken. Nothing could move the audience. Too much nature is unpardonable; too much art is death."

Miss Morris is frequently asked whether she

loses her own identity in the character she plays. Here is a story she tells :

"Once, in New York, when a number of us were at dinner, Mr. Stuart, one of the party, asked me the same thing. I told him to wait until after the play, and he would see if I lost myself in my role. We were very merry at dinner—you know I can be merry—and when it was over, Stuart, who had been laughing uproariously, said, 'You needn't think you can make me cry to-night, after seeing your mirth at this table!' Well, we went to the theatre. The play was 'Miss Multon.' It has a very strong climax. The scene is very forcible. It is brought to a close by *Miss Multon* casting herself, or rather falling upon the floor, very nearly in convulsions. I fell down as usual. I felt the part very acutely. My heart was beating violently, and I was red with excitement. As I lay there, I happened to look at the box overhead. There I saw Stuart. Even in my anguish, I recognized him.

"His nose was red from excessive weeping, and I could distinctly see the tears tracing themselves down his cheeks. I caught his eye, and—yes, I will say it—gave him a very decided wink. He was furious, and made some remark. The audience hissed him, and he went quietly to the back of the box. He has always declared that he would never forgive me for that wink."

Miss Morris says that it is dangerous to be too sympathetic. Nature must be tempered with art. "I must cry in my emotional roles, and feel enough to cry; but I must not cry enough to mumble my words, to redden my nose, or to become hysterical."

Although the actress relies very little upon the attractions of her person, she does not despise dress. She thinks that good clothes have a great deal to do with a part, and she is decidedly correct. Miss Morris, however, deals very artistically with this question. Her motto is not "Worth; *encore* Worth; *toujours* Worth." On one occasion, in the days to which I have before referred, when her stage wardrobe was decidedly meagre, her waiting-maid appeared in a pink silk dress, with lace and diamonds. Miss Morris has never forgotten that. The maid entirely eclipsed the mistress.

Many a maid nowadays would be willing to do the same thing. The question of dress is far too forcibly emphasized. Women who are known to dress well stand far better chances of engagement than those who are not. And it is the same with the men. Visit the dramatic agencies, and you will always hear the same thing : " He is a good dresser "; or " He has an excellent wardrobe." Very few stars appear in plays that give them no opportunity to " dress." Of course, I do not include the Shakespearian actresses. Even playwrights have become aware of the fact that plays without a drawing-room scene, or a reception incident where costumes can be as extravagant as possible, are unwelcome.

Miss Morris can discuss the question of dress as readily as she can those connected with the more important questions of theatrical interests. She has read a great deal, and has digested all that she has read. She studies intricacies very carefully, and does not cast them aside as unnecessary, as many less worthy actresses are inclined to do. The greater the artist, the more willing will he or she be to clutch at every possible hint that may be given.

Miss Morris is always extremely interesting. She understands her profession from its alpha to omega, and is always willing to talk. She has been frequently misrepresented, but it has done her little harm. As I said before, her name in the annals of the American stage is luminous for all time. She should, however, not abide with us until her greatness has become a memory.

ROSINA VOKES.

OCCUPYING a nice little place all by herself on the American stage, her particular line being refined comedy, is Miss Rosina Vokes. She is a charming little lady, as sprightly and amusing in private life, where she is known as Mrs. Cecil Clay, as she is behind the footlights.

Miss Vokes was the daughter of a London costumer, who did a little for Queen Victoria's realms in the way of supplying them with population. Jessie, Victoria, Fred and Rosina were all Vokes', very much of an age, and all dramatic. When managers wanted a child for a play to be produced, they used to go to Mr. Vokes.

"Have you a child of the necessary age?" they would ask.

The proud father would promptly reply:

"I have a child of any age."

"I commenced my stage career," said Miss Vokes, "at the age of three. Perhaps I had better say that I was born in London, October 18, 1858; witness the family Bible, in which the following remarkable entry occurs: 'Rosina Theodosia, third daughter of Frederick Mortimer Stratford Vokes, and Sarah his wife.' I was carried on the stage by Mr. Creswick, the eminent English actor. (I don't mean that he was eminent because he carried me on, but eminent on his own account.) He carried me round his neck, whilst he fought a broad-sword contest with seven villains. I nearly ended the eminent actor's eminent career then and there by hanging on to his wind-pipe with ten small but penetrating fingers. My sister Jessie played all the classical juveniles at the Drury Lane Theatre. The mantle and the rest of the costume descended successively on Victoria and myself. We branched out as the Vokes children in Scotland, and afterwards as the Vokes family, making our first appearance in London in 1870, with the Drury Lane pantomime. We first appeared in America at the Union Square Theatre in the spring of 1872, in 'The Belles of the Kitchen,' and played in this country the best part of five seasons, going back each Christmas for the pantomime at the Drury Lane Theatre. I left the stage in 1877, and when I returned to this country, eight years afterwards, it was with the very different style of plays that we are now presenting. I believed that there was room for some such light and unpretentious, but refined entertainment, and have every reason to be delighted with, and grateful for our reception in all quarters."

Miss Vokes and her husband spend the greater part of their time in this country. They occupy a pleasant little flat in Fifth avenue, and vary flat life with a short sojourn at the St. James Hotel. They travel all over the country, always closing their season in New York. Then they go to England for the summer. Mr. Clay has a house in London which is always rented during his absence here, and a little country place in Devonshire. It is to the Devonshire retreat that Miss Vokes always flies as soon as she gets to England.

"We might as well stay in New York as in London," says Mr. Clay, "barring the humidity."

Miss Vokes is delightfully domesticated. When she is off the stage she forgets all business cares. She is not what the members of the theatrical profession call "shoppy." In fact she can rarely be induced to talk of the theatre at all, and as a rule it is Mr. Clay to whom she refers all visitors. She lives very quietly indeed, and is not in the least eccentric.

Miss Vokes is a hard worker. She directs all rehearsals of plays in which she is to appear, making suggestions from start to finish. Sometimes she produces little comedies, in which her leading actors appear, and in those cases she relies upon the actors themselves, believing that this is the wisest policy, when she can afford to do so. Her great anxiety is that every member of her company shall have a chance. She is one of the most unselfish "stars" that I have ever met. She does not believe in "one-part" plays, and makes it a point to secure comedies that do not rely entirely for success upon her own bright individuality. "A thoroughly good performance all round" is the criticism that is most pleasing to Miss Vokes.

Mr. and Mrs. Clay read about eight hundred plays each year. They are deluged with the efforts of young playwrights, who think it an easy matter to write one-act comedies like those produced by Miss Vokes. But it is a case of the survival only of the fittest.

"We read everything," said Mr. Clay, as we chatted together one afternoon in the lobby of the St. James. "I think it was Talleyrand who remarked that he saw every caller for fear he might miss the man he had been waiting to meet for twenty years. That is our idea. If we did not read all the manuscripts submitted to us, we might lose our greatest chance. We have at the present time a great many more plays, accepted and paid for, than we shall be able to produce."

In studying a part the very last thing Miss Vokes does is to learn the lines. She knows all the points of the play, and the smallest details of the role she is to play, before she has committed to memory a single word. She has completely realized the character before she is able to rehearse it. The songs she introduces are very carefully selected, and on no occasion are they ever completely irrelevant to the play.

After Miss Vokes' retirement from the stage, she used to appear in private theatricals. On one occasion she was a member of an amateur company from which great things were expected. Sir Charles Young and a number of other well-known people were in the cast. There was some difficulty, and Miss Vokes found herself left with these people, all their plans having evaporated. She made contracts with them; the organization was too good a one to lose. She made the company her own, and returned to the stage.

Hundreds of young girls apply to Miss Vokes each year for "advice," and she is always ready to give the best she can. She says that she would like to engage them all, but that of course would be impossible, especially as some of them have nothing to offer the stage but their good looks. Miss Vokes considers a stage career very seriously. She does not believe in adopting it in a patronizing way. Great industry and sincerity she looks upon as absolutely necessary to achieve success. One of her favorite stories is that of the little boy, who, when his papa asked him what he wanted to be when he grew up, replied that his ambition was to become a policeman. The father entertained grave doubts as to his son's success in that walk.

"Well, papa," said the boy "you know that if the worst comes to the worst, I can be an actor."

Two of the members of the old Vokes family are dead—Jessie and Fred. Victoria came to America during the present season (1890) as a star, but did not meet with much success. Fawdon Vokes, who was not a son of the costumer, but merely a Vokes professionally, is still playing in England.

When asked as to her hopes, Miss Vokes

always says: "My ambition—personal ambition, that is—is to do small things well, so that nobody can know that I couldn't do big things well if I tried."

NELLIE McHENRY.

LIKE a draught of champagne is Miss Nellie McHenry, refreshing, invigorating, and more-ish—with a thousand excuses for the last adjective, which I know is not to be found in Webster's Unabridged. She is known in private life as Mrs. John Webster, though, if she take her husband's name, I don't know why she shouldn't be Mrs. "Johnny" Webster. It is not the easiest thing in the world to catch a glimpse of Miss McHenry. It is still more difficult to make her the subject of an interview, as she is generally roaming through the United States. She occasionally plays even through the summer months.

Yet Mr. and Mrs. Johnny Webster have a delightful residence in the Highlands of New Jersey, on the banks of the Shrewsbury river,

and when they are at home —well, they are "at home" with a vengeance. They keep open house as far as their friends are concerned. The house on the Shrewsbury is "Liberty Hall." Mr. and Mrs. Webster are royal entertainers.

In spite of her perpetual peregrination, Miss McHenry is growing stout, and I half suspect that it is owing to this fact that she is anxious to abandon the "rough and tumble" business of the farce-comedy soubrette, and adopt more serious roles. Her manager, Mr. Frank Maeder, informed me that she wanted "lights and shades" and intended to have them, as she believes that more dignified comedy would suit her admirably. So do I.

I had the pleasure of calling upon Miss McHenry when she was playing in New York a few weeks ago, and I put her through her "paces" without any hesitation. She is deliciously unconventional and "free and easy." Miss McHenry doesn't know the meaning of the word "frills" as applied, perhaps rather vulgarly, to manners. She is not at all impressed with the sense of her own importance, and, after all, it *is* rather nice to meet an actress who isn't. There is something of the unusual about them, I am inclined to think. Miss McHenry was in her dressing-room, between the acts of "Green-room Fun," in which she was playing at the Harlem Opera House. She was willingly reminiscent, and my ears—both of them—were more than at her service.

"Sometimes . say to myself," began Miss

McHenry, "when I see all these theatrical surroundings, and feel this play-house atmosphere, that life is a strange thing, after all. I know that is rather a conventional" (Miss McHenry said "chestnutty") "utterance, and I like to be original at times, but it does seem peculiar that a whole career should sometimes hinge upon a mere incident. The most trivial happening is sometimes sufficient to change the whole course of a life. Don't look so impatient. I am making a point. You agree with me, don't you?"

Of course I did. It is my business to agree with everybody, until I have a nice pen and ink in front of me.

"I went upon the stage by the purest accident," said Miss McHenry. "My family was not theatrical. I had no idea of ever earning my living behind the footlights. Listen to an account of the accident: A comedian named Will Wiggins lived in the same house as that occupied by my father and mother. Of course I became acquainted with him. One day I was returning home from school, and who should I meet but the amiable Mr. Wiggins. He asked me where I was going, and I, being a nice, affable, well-behaved school-girl, told him that, as it was a half holiday, I was about to seek some girls I knew, and have a good time.

"'Have you ever been to a theatre?' asked Wiggins.

"I never had. I looked up to Wiggins imploringly. I was longing to go. 'Come along,' he said, and I need not remark that he did not repeat the injunction. I followed him like a little lamb. Mr. Wiggins was going to a rehearsal, he told me. I didn't exactly know what a rehearsal was, so I was silent, not wishing to betray my ignorance. I was not at all impressed with the sight of the theatre. It was dark and gloomy, and so untidy that it gave me a positive pain. Everything seemed to be topsy-turvy. I began to wonder how it could possibly look gay and festive at night, and why people paid so much attention to what seemed to me such an undesirable looking place. The play that they were rehearsing was Octave Feuillet's 'Romance of a Poor Young man.' Lawrence Barrett was to play the leading part. Now comes the accident. Of course you know that a child is needed in 'The Romance of a Poor Young Man,' to play the part of the flower-girl. Well, on this afternoon, the girl was not able to come to the theatre. Her mother was ill, I believe, or something of the kind. Mr. Barrett saw me standing on the stage, and I heard him say to the manager, 'Who is that child?'

"'I don't know,' was the reply. 'I'll find out. Perhaps she can play the flower-girl. I don't believe that the other child knew her part, anyway.'

"I was just a little bit frightened when Lawrence Barrett came up to me and took my hand. He asked me if I could read. That put me on my mettle, and I replied, rather fiercely, that of course I could. Said Lawrence, taking me immediately at my word: 'Well, my little girl, come over here, and read this part for me. Remember that I want you to read it just as though you were talking to one of the little girls with whom you go to school. See if you can do that. You must forget that you are among strange people, and in a strange place. Try to imagine that you are a flower girl. I wonder if you can do it. I don't believe you can.' I didn't believe I could, either, until he uttered those words. They finished me. I was perfectly determined that I would do my very best. I was not afraid any more. Taking up the manuscript, I read deliberately the words that I saw. Since those days, I have wondered at my self-assurance. Lawrence Barrett is, and was, an actor of recognized ability, and very few girls would read a part for the first time before him without some very conspicuous hesitation. When

I had finished, all the people standing around in that dark, cold theatre, clapped their hands and smiled at me. Mr. Barrett patted my cheek. I thought that was very nice of him.

" 'I wonder,' he said, presently, looking at me very carefully, 'if you could learn what you have just read, by heart, and come and act here to-night.'

"I don't remember exactly what I said. He took my breath away, and, at any rate, I could not have been very coherent. A short time afterwards, however, I found myself on my way home with the manuscript in my hand, and, arrived at my domicile, I informed my father and mother that I was going to be an actress, flourishing the manuscript in the air in proof of my statement."

Miss McHenry laughed. I was just going to compliment her on her excellent memory, when I remembered that such a speech might disconcert her. It would sound as though the events she had just described were very far off, whereas an actress' memory is not supposed to go back farther than ten years, at least while she is still before the public.

"The first thing I did," she resumed, "when I had taken off my things, was to go before the glass in my bed-room and pose. How I posed! I was intensely dramatic, and I flourished away as though my life depended upon it. I found no difficulty in committing the part to memory. By dinner-time I was letter-perfect, as we say in the profession. Well, I sat down to dinner, and was hungry enough to forget my dramatic aspirations for half an hour. As soon as the meal was over, I flew to my book, and imagine my horror and grief when I found that I had forgotten a great many of the lines. I burst out crying. My father and mother, who were not too pleased with Mr. Wiggins, wanted to take the book from me, but I had told Mr. Barrett that I could act the part at night, and I was determined that nothing should interfere with my doing so. I dried my tears and began to study again, and once more I was letter-perfect. Then I set out for the theatre, and arrived there long before I was due. I went through the part again and again, and they told me, at last, that the performance was about to begin. Then it was that I grew frightened. I wished most devoutly that I had not had a half holiday. I blessed the unfortunate Mr. Wiggins for ever having made the acquaintance of my father and mother. I wondered how it would all end. My heart beat violently, my legs trembled; I was so nervous that I couldn't keep still. Mr. Barrett must have seen my agony; it was visible to the most casual observer.

"'Don't be afraid, Nellie,' he said, kindly. 'You have nothing to fear. Just forget that there are any people in the house, and speak your lines perfectly naturally, just as though you were talking to your friends. If you ever become an actress, remember what I say. It will serve you in good stead.'

"And it has," continued Miss McHenry. "But to proceed with my narrative. I knew nothing about 'cues' and other theatrical phrases. I didn't even know when I had to go upon the stage. Somebody who was standing by my side whispered to me, 'Now it is your turn, Nellie; go on the stage like a brave girl, and say your lines, then turn round, and come off.' I shall never forget that moment. It was simply awful. But I was in for it, and I remember resolving to do my very best. So I made my first appearance, before what they call in the penny dreadfuls 'a sea of faces.' I never missed a word. I was surprised at myself. It really seemed easy after all. The company treated me very kindly, and I received many words of praise. And that is how I first went on the stage."

It was certainly interesting, and the actress

related the incident as though she thoroughly enjoyed the reminiscence.

"And afterwards?" I asked.

"Oh," she said, "the afterwards was the tug of war. You see I liked my first appearance with the stage, and determined that I would be an actress. But there were not so very many plays then with children in them. I used to rush up to Mr. De Bar, the manager, every time I met him in the street. 'When can I play again?' I would ask. Mr. De Bar was a good-natured fellow, but he used to chaff me mercilessly. His favorite reply to my demand was, 'Oh, go home, Nellie, and grow. You're such a bit of a thing.' That made me very angry. Of course I was a bit of a thing, but I couldn't help that, and I thought it was very cruel of him to be always throwing my size and age in my teeth. But he hadn't forgotten me, by any means. My next appearance was due to another accident. Charlotte Thompson was playing in the city, and the child in her company fell ill. Mr. De Bar at once sent for me. It seems dreadful to think that my two first engagements were due to somebody's illness, doesn't it? But it is a fact. I learned my lines like a little heroine, and was not in the least nervous. But I had a terrible experience, one that would disconcert me even now, when I have done a great deal of knocking around in the theatrical world. I had to make my appearance in the second act, and utter a little speech all by myself, after which Miss Thompson was to come upon the stage and interrupt me. Well, I made my little speech very nicely, I am quite sure. Then I looked around for Miss Thompson. She was not forthcoming. I didn't know what to do. I almost wished that the stage would open and swallow me up. But it didn't. Think what a horrible position I was in. I said my speech all over again. No Miss Thompson made her appearance. I repeated it once more; the audience grew impatient; there was a hum of disapproval. At last she came, looking furious. I shall never forget the anger that shot from her eyes. By this time I was quite beside myself. I had lost all idea of the play. Miss Thompson's appearance upset me. I went all through my part as though it were a connected recitation, and as if nobody had a right to interrupt me. I will leave you to imagine the utter chaos that I caused. The act was ruined, and—well, I will also leave you to imagine what kind of a reception I had behind the scenes."

Miss McHenry had many other bright anecdotes to tell. Since the days of which she spoke she has been a member of Barney McAuley's company, and of the stock company at Hooley's Theatre, Chicago. It was there that she met Nate Salsbury, and with him she started in the organization known as the Salsbury Troubadours.

Miss McHenry's husband, Mr. Webster, always appears on the stage with her. A sister,

Miss Tillie McHenry, also became a member of the profession, but has retired. But Nellie goes through the country year after year, bringing laughter in her wake, and leaving the influence of her own bright personality with every audience that welcomes her. Her art may not be of a very lofty kind; her methods may not be always worthy of serious criticism. But, as I said at the beginning of this sketch, Miss McHenry is like a draught of champagne, refreshing, invigorating, and more-ish.

www.ingramcontent.com/pod-product-compliance
Lightning Source LLC
Chambersburg PA
CBHW032144010526
44111CB00035B/1118